The Book of Horses and Horsemanship

by Jeff Griffen

illustrated by Jeanne Mellin

Prentice-Hall, Inc., Englewood Cliffs, N. J.

The author wishes to thank Mr. and Mrs. Clifton L. Havener Jr., Quarter Horse and Morgan enthusiasts, and Dr. Howard C. Raven, veterinarian, for their valuable assistance and comments, and also to thank Miss Tere Vanario, well-known riding instructress, Mrs. Audrey Kingery, one of the East's leading barrel racers, and Wayne Bonnel, for help in demonstrating proper mounting technique.

This book is dedicated to horse lovers, past and present, in whose hands man's most noble animal has prospered, and especially to future horse lovers whose duty will be to maintain him as our civilization ever changes.

Contents

Introduction

IT IS ALWAYS A WELCOME EXPERIENCE TO READ A BOOK whose author knows what he is talking about. Sometimes this results from a short period of intensive study and research; sometimes it results from a careful and conscientious review of other pertinent writing on the same subject; and sometimes—as in this book by Jeff Griffen—it results from a lifetime of interest and first-hand experience.

Jeff Griffen's lifetime has been comparatively short, but much of his thirty-odd years has been spent dealing with horses, their breeding, training, showing, and most important, their continued function as part of the American tradition.

Horse literature grows every day because the public interest is itself persistent, and constantly increasing.

I believe one can fairly say that horses are playing a wider and broader role in our society every day.

Horsemanship is one of the performing arts, recognized as such for centuries in continental Europe, the Middle East, and northern Africa, and in America since Colonial times. In a larger sense, the art, whether perfected or not, provides rewards in discipline, patience and self-control, and in the transmittal of those qualities to a horse. But this is not the end of the story, however, because there is a further reward, which is the enjoyment and pleasure of working with an animal, as contrasted with, let us say, working with a machine.

I doubt that anyone who is remotely interested in the horse or in horsemanship can do better than to read Jeff Griffen's book, which should be a stimulating experience, whether the reader be young or old. And I predict that the reward of that reading will also be enjoyment. Finally, I commend this book to the many hundreds of professional horsemen as an aid to their able guidance of the young Americans whose interest in horses and horsemanship will sustain the art, and who will gain its rewards.

JAMES A. THOMAS, JR.
Director, National Horse Show Association

1.

The horse
is not doomed

FOR MORE THAN THIRTY YEARS NOW EXPERTS HAVE BEEN saying that there is no place left for the horse in our modern society. They serve up figures to show how he has been robbed of farm work by the tractor, outmoded as transportation by the auto, bus, plane and train, no longer able to compete with trucks and trailers, gone from the cavalry as a result of military mechanization. Even blacksmithing is becoming a forgotten profession, they cry.

For the benefit of those people who love horses, let it be said that this dreary picture is not accurate. The heavy draft horse, which comprised the vast majority of the equine population in the United States before World War II, is dead. But the light horse, used primarily for riding, racing, show-rodeo competition and ranch work, has made startling growth. The Thoroughbred, Standardbred, Saddle Horse, Arabian, Quarter Horse, Morgan, Tennessee Walker and Appaloosa, all light breeds, are providing pleasure for hundreds of thousands of people young and old throughout the country, as well as profit for many others associated with the exciting world of horses.

How big is this growth? In 1962 the horse was the sole support of a near-$4-billion industry ranging from vitamins to saddlery. A large share of this included race-track betting, but it took the horse to make the race. Right now there are more professional trainers, jockeys and registered horses than ever before in the history of our country. Almost as many veterinarians are engaged full or part time in horse treatment as in the entire dairy industry. Several universities offer courses in horse raising, management and/or riding. One college is entirely devoted to equine teaching. The student begins his or her freshman year with a weanling, and during the four-year course, as the foal becomes a mature horse, all aspects of its growth, care, training and handling are studied. Nor is blacksmithing a profession of the past. Three colleges offer courses in this line, and graduated farriers are able to go forth into a lucrative future of outdoor work paying as high as $20,000 to $25,000 annually.

No, the horse is far from doomed. He has been used differently in the past twenty years. Today he is an animal of pleasure and competition, always well cared for, often magnificently trained. He rides around the country in small trailers attached to the rears of autos and flies coast to coast or even overseas. Old breeds have been refined, new ones developed and registries established everywhere, even for the near-extinct mustang, pride and spirit of the West. More likely than not, a good horse nowadays will have a pedigree.

What does riding or showing or training a horse mean? It may be just enjoying the solitude of the great outdoors free from the rush of cars and people, cantering to the brow of the next hill, or watching a sunset as your horse ambles slowly homeward. It may be joining a posse or trail-riding club of friendly people and packing off into the wilderness for a weekend. Or it may be in a show ring when you turn your rugged jumper slowly and aim him at a six-foot barrier, feel him lengthen his stride, pick up speed, coil and leap, up and over cleanly, then down and on to the next one. It may be a five-gaited Saddle Horse in a prancing trot, ears spiked forward, legs whipping up in spirited animation, a keg of rhythmic dynamite under you. It may be a barrel-racing event or a cutting class or a precision-drill group or a long parade past thousands of people, bands playing and you in an Indian or Arab costume. By owning, training and competing with a horse, a young person

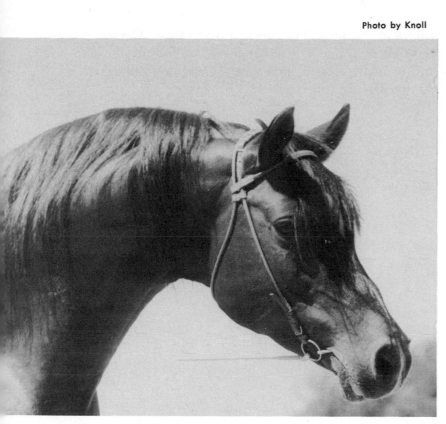

Arabian champion Imaraff

gains a sense of responsibility, of courage and good sportsmanship—the thrill of winning, the art of losing gracefully but trying again. These are the values needed to counterbalance the mechanical side of modern life.

The horse is flesh and blood on a noble scale. He has strength, beauty, spirit, ability to learn and is superbly functional—all reasons why the greatest men throughout history have taken inordinate pride in their mounts. Seldom do you look at a horse and laugh. If he is old and swayback or of peculiar conformation, you may, but when he is well put together and his coat is glistening, his muscles rippling and head alert in proud carriage, there comes a quickening to the human heart.

The world of horses is a satisfying and healthy world for the energetic person, yet one which has its requirements. For the horse more than ever before is dependent upon man. Though he does not ask for the pampering he usually receives nowadays, neither can he stand to be abused or neglected. To own one means care and responsibility, but the satisfaction he will return will outweigh tenfold the effort required to keep him. The experience will compound itself in fair play and respect for both men and animals for the remainder of your life, for there is something about a good horse that makes a man good too.

The purpose of this book is to introduce everyone to this exciting and rewarding world of horses. All the breeds and their various uses will be discussed, as well as care and handling, basic riding English and Western style, the clothes to wear, the tack to use, and how to build a one-horse stable. Any person possessing a deep love for the horse can rightfully consider a lifetime career in this field. The opportunity is there. One need only be imaginative and hardworking, for the horse's future is destined to grow bigger, brighter and better in the years to come.

2.
Some
horse sense

Anyone interested in the horse should know something about his origins, for in the case of *Equus,* as science calls him, one of the most interesting evolutions in all the animal kingdom has been unearthed and pieced together. This is at times hard to believe, but it is nevertheless accurate because there are almost no missing links.

The first horse of which there is record lived around sixty million years ago in the *Eocene* Age. Labeled *Eohippus,* or Dawn Horse, he had four toes on his front feet and three on his back, each tipped with a tiny hoof. He was about twelve inches in height at the shoulder, the size of a fox, and could run like the wind. His speed

5

and darting maneuverability were the key to survival in an age of saber-toothed tigers and other prehistoric mammals.

Eohippus fossil remains were first uncovered in New Mexico in 1876, and later in several other areas of the world, such as South America, Asia and Europe around London and Paris, attesting to the fact that this doughty little animal just about covered the earth. But only in the North American hemisphere did he evolve. Elsewhere he died out. Here, through the eons of time, he became *Mesohippus,* the Mid-way horse, gaining size to that of a collie, and carrying more weight on his center toe until it became a sturdy hoof. He changed to *Merychippus* with an advance in tooth construction that allowed him to masticate tough grass and move form the forest to the plain; then *Pliohippus,* in which the extra toes became splint bones buried under the leg skin, where they remain today in our horse *Equus,* developed and evolved in North America. The fossil beds of Texas and Nebraska, the desert caves of Arizona, the famous asphalt beds at Rancho La Brea, California, and other places up to Alaska have yielded the bones of *Equus,* the first true horse, showing that vast herds existed in those times.

Then came the Ice Age and *Equus* began to roam or was driven by the great seas of ice which covered most of the continent. With the llama he crossed the newly risen Isthmus of Panama into South America. With the then-diminutive camel he crossed the Bering Peninsula, which at that time was the land link to Asia. From there he spread into the far reaches of Europe and Africa. In time several different species arose—wild asses, zebras and onagers, from pony height horses to large draft-size animals.

So the American horse wandered until he covered the earth, except for isolated areas like Australia. Then came the great horse death in North and South America. They all succumbed. No one knows why. Perhaps all their fodder was destroyed by an Ice Age winter, but the less intelligent, less agile buffalo survived. More likely a truculent disease of epidemic proportions wiped them out, and, since the watery Bering Strait had by this time formed, none of the Asian stock could return.

Though the horse came to an end in the Western Hemisphere, he thrived elsewhere. We know large herds existed in Europe and were vital to the existence of early man. On the walls of caves in southern France are beautiful pictures of horses painted by Cro-Magnon man twenty thousand years ago. Man at that time hunted the horse for food, and nearby are great Cro-Magnon trash heaps, one of which contains the bones of over a hundred thousand horses.

Sometime after this, man domesticated the horse, probably when a colt was captured by some children. Once grown, it was put to use by adults and found extremely valuable in hauling and carrying articles from camp site to camp site. Later, when the wheel was invented, chariots, wagons, carts and sleds were made, and the horse was ridden.

Many historians have said that the utilization of the horse was one of the great turning points in civilization. The horse made man mobile in a thousand different ways, allowed him to stretch his brain to plan and create, whether it was crossing a vast desert, plowing a field or charging into war. All the great military conquests of history until 1941 have utilized the horse to an amazing degree. The Persians conquered the Middle East astride hundreds of thousands of horses. Alexander the Great conquered the then-known world by superb military tactics involving foot soldiers and cavalry. He rode a black stallion named Bucephalus which he loved so deeply that when it died he named a city in Persia after it. The Arabs spread Islam by the sword and the horse. Thousands of heavily armored knights on great horses went on the Crusades to battle Mohammedans on light horses. Chivalry of the Middle Ages, when knighthood reached its peak in honor and pageantry, comes from the French word *cheval,* meaning horse. The Duke of Wellington directed the Battle of Waterloo from the back of his famous charger Copenhagen, and defeat was prevented no less than five times by cavalry thrusts.

And America herself owes an unending debt of gratitude to the horse for the role it played in founding our country. The Spanish conquistadors brought the horse back to the Western Hemisphere in the early 16th century and within a hundred years descendants of their escaped Jennets and Barbs were roaming the plains in great herds. The Quarter-Mile Running Horse, the Narragansett Pacer and the Justin Morgan all played their part in the early life of the colonies. Pack horses opened up Pennsylvania and Kentucky and Ohio when there were only paths in these areas. Teams of mighty Percherons hauled prairie schooners westward, then plowed the sod for wheat. The Civil War horse, the Pony Express, the cow pony, all are an intimate part of our heritage. It is no wonder that today, when we have made our lives more mobile, more mechanical, more complex, we turn back to the horse. Just when logic deems we should eliminate him from our life as an essentially useless item, we find other ways to use him—for new kinds of competition and for real pleasure and companionship. A horse is good for a man, just as much now as he ever was.

No special language is used in the horse world, but there are many terms which would be confusing if you were to engage a horseman in a spirited conversation. Not all the terms can be covered here but the basic ones are listed along with some general information.

A horse's height is the vertical distance from the ground to the highest point of his withers (area above his front legs—see diagram). The unit for measuring height is the "hand," which is 4 inches. Thus when someone nods at a horse and says, "He's about 15-2," it means he's 15 hands and 2 inches tall, or 62 inches, which is average horse size. A horse of 16 hands is on the large side; if he is 17-2, as some draft horses and an occasional hunter reach, he is a near giant. If he is 14-2 or under, he is classified as a pony.

Old-timers can judge a horse's height at a glance. They know the exact number of inches from their eye level to the ground and by standing beside a horse's front limbs and looking at the top of the withers they usually guess right on the button.

Ponies weigh from 400 to 900 pounds, light horses 900 to 1400, draft horses 1400 and up, with a big Shire occasionally going to 2300 or 2500 pounds.

The average age of a horse is twenty to twenty-five years, though they often live to be thirty-five and over. Generally their teeth, which wear off as they eat but continually rise from the gums so a perfect bite is maintained, last until they are thirty years old or more.

Horses come in many colors: bay, brown, chestnut, black, gray, roan, white, dun, buckskin, piebald and skewbald. Strawberry roan and flea-bitten gray are reputable colors. A horse with a "white stocking" is one that has a white leg to the knee or above; "white sock" means white below the knee.

A horse when first born is called a foal. After the foal is weaned from its dam, or mother, at about six months of age, it is called a weanling. After its first year it is a yearling; after its second year, a two-year-old. A young male horse is a colt. He is raced as a two-year-old if he happens to be a Thoroughbred; is never pleasure ridden or Western-trained until his third year, and then only lightly because his back is not strong enough to support much weight. He doesn't lose his last milk teeth (baby teeth) or reach full maturity until his fifth year.

A young female horse is called a filly and holds this title until she is four years old. After that time she is referred to as a mare. The gestation period for a mare is eleven months.

An adult male horse is a stallion. A gelding is a male horse which has been castrated before he reached maturity. He is generally more passive and more easily handled in the company of other horses than a stallion. A stallion castrated after he has reached maturity is called a stag. Practically all male race horses are stallions because if they become outstanding winners they are extremely valuable at stud in perpetuating the breed.

The official birthday of all registered horses is January 1 of each year. This is done to simplify records, classes and races, particularly for younger horses. A colt or filly born in December must compete against those born earlier that same year, but most foals are born in the spring, when the weather is nice and the summer lies ahead. Late foals are the exception, not the rule, among horse breeders.

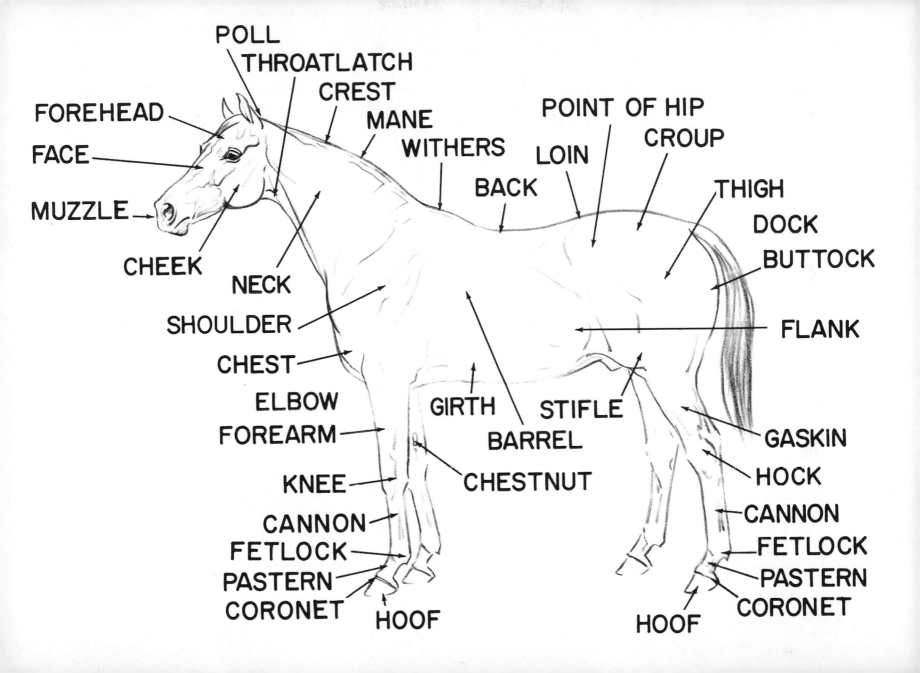

In Thoroughbred circles the term "cold blood" is heard frequently. A Thoroughbred is considered hot-blooded, and when he is crossed out of Thoroughbred lines, be it to registered or unregistered stock, this is referred to as cold blood. Thoroughbred breeders claim that in no instance has the infusion of cold blood added to the speed, spirit and high competitive nature of the Thoroughbred.

Whenever you come across an asterisk before a horse's name in reading or on a pedigree (for example, Rex Ellsworth's famous stallion *Khaled), it means that the horse was imported. This applies only to Thoroughbred blood but is often seen in Standardbred, even Quarter Horse pedigrees tracing back to early foundation stock, much of which was the finest English Thoroughbred.

Often the term "grade" is used as in a Grade Morgan or Grade Arab. This refers to a horse with some Morgan or Arab blood in him and consequently some of the characteristics of the breed, but he is not eligible for registration.

Around halter classes people often say that a certain horse is "typie," or true to type. It means that his conformation is close to the standards of the breed and usually on the flashy or refined side.

The gaits of a horse are the various ways he moves at different speeds and can be either natural or taught. The principal gaits are walk, trot and canter in equitation riding; walk, jog and lope in Western riding. The run, or gallop, is simply a fast canter. Certain breeds of horses have special gaits which will be discussed as we proceed.

The diagram lists the important parts and areas of the horse. Eyes, ears, tail, etc., have not been labeled because we believe people have intelligence too.

3.
The Arabian

THE OLDEST PURE BREED OF HORSE ON EARTH, EASIEST TO keep, possessed with remarkable endurance, intelligence, gentleness, spirit and beauty, prime contributor to just about every light-horse breed in the world—this is the Arabian.

It is difficult not to overpraise this 14- to 15½-hand little horse which weighs only 750 to 1000 pounds. He is quality and toughness combined with flaming vitality. He loves people, is a big ham at heart, and treats children as the neighborhood dog would. Climb up on his back and he swells with pride. His neck bows, his tail goes up and he's ready to gallop for miles. You don't "break" an Arabian, you train him. He rebels against brutality, even fights it. Challenge his intelli-

11

Arabian mare, Ducaseyn Du, owned by Oren S. Ackley

gence, dare him to do something, and he's there with everything he has.

And a lot he has, too. He has given his remarkable breathing apparatus, his big lungs and heart and strong legs to the Thoroughbred. He's given class and strength, the bowed neck and dish face to the Morgan. He's given the proud gaiety, the high tail and alert ears to the American Saddle Horse and Tennessee Walker. He's given the trotter and pacer its endurance. To the Quarter Horse he's given speed and intelligence which through the years has come to be called "cow savvy."

What is the origin of this great little horse? No one really knows.

Myth has it that Ishmael captured a wild mare about 2000 B.C. and she foaled a stallion which began the first strain of pure Arabs known as *Kuhaylan*. Another story tells of a sheik being hotly pursued by his enemies across the desert. Eventually he had to stop to rest his war mare and in this moment she gave birth to a filly foal. Forced to continue, he remounted the mare and pushed on. When he finally reached a town and stopped, he was startled to discover the young filly had followed. He gave her to an old woman and she grew up to found another strain of Arab, *Kuhaylan 'Ajuz*, known as The Old Woman's Mare.

Another legend concerns Salaman, who lived about 1635 B.C. After a long three-day ride across the desert without water, Salaman and his warriors spotted an oasis and dismounted. The thirst-crazed mares smelled water and stampeded toward the wells. An ambush was feared so the trumpeter blew assembly—the call by which the mares had been trained to return to their riders. Only five out of the herd obeyed, but because of their intrepid loyalty they were bred to the greatest stallions obtainable and thus was founded the present-day Arabian of five basic strains and a thousand off-shoots.

The paradox of all these myths is that historically the Arab was one of the last people on earth to acquire the horse, probably a few years after the birth of Christ. If the Arabian had existed as an outstanding breed much before that, the Greeks would certainly have found and used it. The Greeks were superb horsemen, and maintained a great racing center on the island of Chios from 400 to 100 B.C. Here they carefully crossed strong Thracean stallions with the swift little mares of Thessaly, brought horse training, chariot racing and flat racing to the height of perfection. Alexander the Great, as he conquered the world (the Middle East today), sent back Scythian stallions and Persian mares to upgrade his cavalry and cross into racers at Chios. But there was no mention of an Arabian horse.

Pegasus, the legendary Greek flying horse, was supposed to have been foaled in western Libya. The Greeks

Arabian champion under English saddle

13

had the highest respect for Libyan horses, which history later called Barbs.

The Barb and Arabian are very similar horses in quality and beauty, close enough to be cousins, if not blood brothers. The Barb is slightly larger, not quite as symmetrical, but neither has he been kept so pure as the Arabian. Some believe the Arabian to be descended from Oriental war horses which charged out of the Khyber Pass and across the plains from India. But more believe he came from the deserts of western Libya, the place of origin of the noble Pegasus.

What has kept the Arabian pure for these many centuries when all other manner of horse breeds have come and gone and been changed by man?

It is the fanatic loyalty and devotion of the Arab to his horse. To understand it one must understand the Arab's lonely existence. The desert offers unrelenting cruelty. Forage is very scarce, water holes miles apart. Neighbors are brutal tribes that attack by day or night. A swift horse that can survive and be useful in this environment is a precious jewel. To maintain and perpetuate it in all purity is imperative. Arabic songs celebrate a thousand times over war mares who have saved their owners' lives. The mating of a noble mare to a great stallion calls for a feast and the exchanging of gifts. Records are not kept but everyone remembers for generations back the breeding of pure Arabians. Those which have a taint of outside blood are never used for breeding. If a mare is accidentally bred to impure blood, she can never be used for breeding pure bloods again. The Arab takes a lovely foal into his tent, but never dogs, which he detests. He is intensely proud of the width of his horse's forehead, *Jibbah,* for it denotes intelligence. He is proud of the *Mitbah,* the manner of excellence by which the head joins the neck. In the eternal struggle with the desert and other tribes, chicanery is always necessary, but with horses one must be scrupulously honest. There is never any question about that. Nor is there ever any question about selling one's best horse. Money means nothing when it is a matter of life or death. You never sell it. Thus the best blood of the desert horse has always been there—maintained over the centuries by love, by song, by religion, by necessity.

But in the last ten years a strange thing has begun to happen. As change sweeps the world it reaches even into the lives of the Arabian people. They begin to want cars instead of horses, houses instead of tents. Today the Bedouins still raise horses but there are signs that their grandchildren may not. For this reason the bastion of the Arabian horse is fast becoming America. It has some 15,000 pure, registered Arabians, almost as many as Arabia itself and more than the rest of the world combined. The number has doubled in the last decade and is expected to double again in the next. The Arabian here may not be bred with the fanatic culling that has

Two Arabian National Champions, Synbad and Mujahid, say "Hello!"

long taken place in its desert home, but the U.S. registry in Chicago has been closed since its inception in 1907. When registration books are closed, it means that no outcrossing is permitted, hence the Arabians in America are as pure as those in their homeland. The horses being bred here today are cared for with the same love and devotion. Judging schools are being held so neophytes can learn and appreciate the qualities of the Arabian.

The principal reasons for the Arabian's rise in popularity are its beauty, personality and wide versatility.

The Arabian is noted for his distinctive head. He is dished, with his forehead extremely wide and bright eyes set nearly halfway between the poll and muzzle, thus providing a lot of brain room. His profile scoops in and his face tapers elegantly to the muzzle. The Arabian's neck is also distinctive in the way it curves grace-fully, yet with great force, into the withers. His chest and barrel are wide, his back is short. The fact that the Arabian has one less vertebra in his back than other horses enables him to carry heavy weight though he is small. His knees and hocks are strongly constructed, his feet on the large side and tough. The tail, third distinctive feature of the Arabian, is carried with swishing gaiety, particularly at the gallop, for which the Arabian is famous. It is his most beautiful gait, breathtaking to watch, never pounding, just an easy endless roll.

The Arabian's walk is unusual in that it is quite fast and the rear foot overreaches the front anywhere from 12 to 30 inches. His trot is a bit uncomfortable because he throws his feet out rather than picks them up with the high action of a Saddle Horse, but it too is an attractive gait.

Contrary to popular belief, the Arab does not fancy

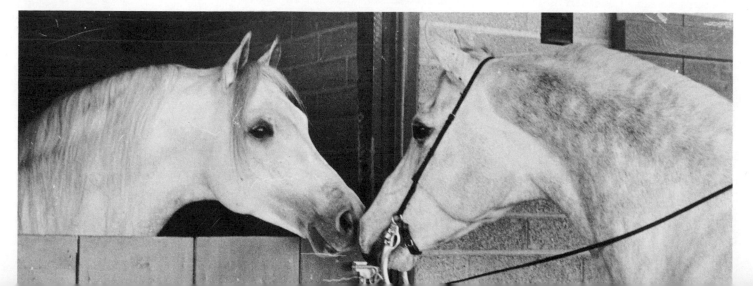

a white horse, or a black one either. Although both are acceptable colors, he considers them unequal to dark bays and dark chestnuts. Steel grays, which are often covered with dapples, are considered good, but lighter colors and piebalds represent impure breeding.

Never has there been an Arabian that was a hay-burner. For centuries they have survived on little food and water, and this trait is still with them.

In personality the Arabian is highly spirited but not vicious. He frisks and plays in the joy of living. Through centuries of intimate companionship with his Bedouin master the Arabian has become inculcated with real affection. In Arabia the horse has been known to neigh warnings to his master of approaching strangers or danger. During a battle the war mare will defend her master with fury, and if the rider is wounded, she will stand guard over him. Such traits lead naturally to a companionability not found in many other horses.

Though docile, the Arabian is not the ideal mount for an inexperienced rider. Under saddle he is a considerable amount of horse and it takes a considerable amount of rider to handle him properly and gain his respect. You *ride* an Arabian. You don't clown on him. That is why the owner of an Arabian is an accomplished horseman or woman, in which case he is easy to control and a pleasure to handle.

As for versatility, the all-Arabian horse shows which have sprung up around the country include classes for

An Arabian winner

Champion Arabian mare being ridden sidesaddle

Hunters, Jumpers, Equatation, English and Western Pleasure, Trail Horse, Combination, Dressage, Fine Harness, Cutting, Roping and Gymkhana events, and recently racing at 2½ miles has been added. More than likely an Arabian will compete in several events.

The problem of the all-purpose horse is that he does many things but few of them outstandingly. Not so the Arab. He excels at dressage. He is an excellent cutting horse because he learns quickly and is intrigued by the game of the constantly shifting cow. He is a fine reining horse because he is short-coupled, amazingly agile, quick on his turns and dramatic in movement.

In trail-riding competition the Arabian seems to have no equal. Here his endurance comes to the fore and his amazing sure-footedness makes him ideal over rough mountain trails. He has twice won the nationally famous Roundup Riders of the Rockies Eight-Day Ride in Colorado. He has consistently won another of the country's great endurance rides, the Tevis Cup 100-Mile One-Day Ride from Lake Tahoe to Auburn, California. The 1961 winner was an Arabian, Chagatai, ridden by Drucella Barner. Weighing 870 pounds, this tough little horse carried his 150-pound load the full hundred miles of mountain and desert trails in 13 hours and 2 minutes with only three one-hour rest stops along the way. He did the last 21 miles in 1 hour and 45 minutes. In 1962 Arabians won eight out of eight major

willingness . . .

endurance rides, including the Western States 100-Mile One-Day Ride and the Jim Shoulders 100-Mile One-Day Ride, and also rides in Virginia, Ohio and Long Island.

Surprisingly, several western ranches have been using Arabians and horses of high Arabian blood for general ranch and cattle work for many years. Some individual ranchers imported their own blood, while much of the stock dates back to Arabian stallions placed in the west by the Army Remount Service. Owners and ranchhands alike have high praise for the working Arabian. He is in-

pride . . .

interest . . .

19

telligent, easy to keep, and again his endurance excels.

The Half-Arabian and Anglo-Arabian are both popular and proven horses. Many of the finest jumpers of Europe's Olympic Equestrian teams have been predominantly Arabian, also the mounts of the Canadian and Mexican teams. In the United States these crosses are popular as hunters and pleasure horses.

The Half-Arabian is a horse that has one parent of pure Arabian blood. The other parent can be of any extraction. The Anglo-Arabian is similar, but the off-blood is Thoroughbred. Many years ago the Army Remount Service started a registry for the Half-Arabian and it is being maintained by the International Arabian Horse Association. There are well over twelve thousand Half-Arabians in the country today.

One of the interesting aspects of the Arabian is that his followers are mostly one-, two- or three-horse people. There are almost no large breeders mass-producing Arabians as has happened in other cases. The shows are attended mostly by enthusiastic amateurs who deeply love their horses and develop them to the fullest possible use.

The Arabian is on the verge of a popularity explosion, one that may make this country his new home. It couldn't happen to a gamer, better or more exciting horse.

4.
The
Thoroughbred

Ask any breeder, owner or trainer of Thoroughbreds, any jockey, stable boy, steward or two-dollar bettor and he'll tell you that a good race horse needs more than speed and stamina. He must have "heart."

What do they mean?

The name of the little Thoroughbred was Chase Me. As a colt he was given to a twelve-year-old girl in Maryland who wanted a jumper, so the horse was trained to jump. But his speed was so phenomenal that they decided to give the horse a chance on the flat. He won immediately, first one race, then another, and another, and moved from cheap company right to the top. In 1937 he started in the Metropolitan Handicap against such Thoroughbred greats as Equipoise and Mr. Khyyam. Chase Me was winning the race when only a few strides from the end he faltered, but he gathered himself up and made a final thrust which carried him past the finish line. Then he stood in agony, a broken foreleg dangling, and had to be destroyed on the track while thousands wept openly.

Gameness, courage, the will to win—these make up the "heart" which is in every Thoroughbred.

Like nearly all our modern breeds, the Thoroughbred is a man-made horse. That is, he was created for the special purpose of racing by crossing different breeds. As in most other cases of the horse, man improved on nature.

The American Thoroughbred is a direct descendant of the English Thoroughbred, which was established in the seventeenth and eighteenth centuries by the royalty of England, hence the phrase "Sport of Kings." Arabian and Barb stallions were crossed with Royal mares, which were a blend of Oriental and northern European stock. The swiftest were always bred to each other, thus the modern race horse evolved. All English and American Thoroughbreds trace back to three great stallions: the Byerly Turk, the Darley Arabian and the Godolphin Arabian, or Barb (historians don't know which he was).

The Byerly Turk was brought to England in about 1684 by a Captain Byerly, who obtained the horse from a Turkish officer while fighting in the Balkans. He used the horse as a charger in the Irish wars, then brought it back to England, where it gained fame as a sire. The Byerly Turk line is noted for stamina and fiery spirit. It founded the Cleveland Bays and Hackneys in England, produced the great Herod, first pillar of Thoroughbred bloodlines, and Denmark, which was the foundation sire of the American Saddle Horse, also the Diomed and Sir Archy lines in England and the renowned *Epinard here. Great hunters and jumpers have come from Byerly Turk blood, including old Ugly, the U.S. Cavalry horse which for years thrilled spectators at Madison Square Garden by jumping circles around the opposition.

The Darley Arabian was bought in Aleppo, Syria, by a Mr. Darley and sent to England in 1710. He was a magnificent Arabian, and the line he founded is famous for its beauty of conformation and lightning speed, but it lacks stamina. They are fine for a short haul, not for distances. This line produced Eclipse, the second Thoroughbred pillar, generally considered the greatest race horse of all time, and also contributed to the Hackney. Here in America the Darley Arabian line, through *Justin Morgan, *Bellfounder, *Messenger, and his inbred descendant Hambletonian, founded the Standardbred, which is today's trotter and pacer, and also contributed heavily to the Saddle Horse and the Tennessee Walker.

Stayer—poses himself for the long haul; is longer legged, more stringy in conformation

Sprinter—runs wide open from the start; lasts for shorter distances; is chunky and muscled in conformation

The Godolphin Arabian (or Barb) was purchased in 1724 in Paris; some say from a flower cart, others say from the court stables of Louis XIV, which is more likely. The horse was probably a Barb coming from the Sultan Moulay Ismail, the hashish-crazed ruler of Morocco who was constantly giving away magnificent Barb horses as peace offerings to the kings of Europe from his twelve-thousand-horse stud farm near Meknes.

Known for its endurance and weight-carrying ability, the Godolphin line is studded with great names from Matchem, the third Thoroughbred pillar, right down to the present day, in England, the United States, France, Argentina; anywhere on earth where Thoroughbred horses are raced. Some of the greats here are Spendthrift and Lexington, a horse of the Civil War era who produced 264 winners and led the sire's list of winners sixteen times, seven of them in consecutive years, and also sired the Fair Play line, which produced the immortal Man O' War, War Admiral, Battleship, Stymie and many others.

These lines have been crossed back and forth so much that most Thoroughbreds carry the blood of all three original sires, plus some Quarter Horse also.

In colonial days a great stallion would be shipped

23

Prepping for the Man O' War

over from England and bred to local hot blood, which consisted of Quarter-Mile-Running horses, the popular racers of our early times. By 1850 tastes had changed to longer races of the four-mile variety. When the first Stud Book was begun about that time, several known Quarter Horse mares were listed as foundation stock. In 1893 the American Jockey Club was formed and it took over the task of registration.

As you can see, it is impossible not to talk bloodlines or pedigrees when discussing race horses. Many people spend their lives in such study, but in the final analysis one never knows from paper what kind of offspring two horses will produce. Usually, good horses come from good parents, those with superior bloodlines and outstanding track records. But as soon as someone makes such a statement, along comes a sensational Alsab by an unheard-of stallion out of a ninety-dollar mare. When a sire and dam produce an outstanding horse, it is called a *nick*, and the cross is repeated year after year in the hope that other greats will follow.

There is some confusion about the term "Thoroughbred." A Thoroughbred is a pedigreed, registered breed of horse used for flat racing, steeplechasing, fox hunting and jumping. The word should always be capitalized. The mixup comes when people use it incorrectly to mean "purebred." For many years the U.S. Government kept Thoroughbreds at its remount posts throughout the country. Farmers or anyone who wished could bring

his mares and breed to excellent-blooded stallions. This improved the local stock. In fact the Thoroughbred has had an influence second only to the Arabian in upgrading all breeds of light horses from polo ponies to today's Quarter Horse. Through the years breeders and horse traders began to call anything "thoroughbred," hopefully trying to gain a higher price. Thus confusion was compounded. There are such horses as half-, three-quarter-, even seven-eighth-Thoroughbred, but these are not eligible for registration by the Jockey Club, hence they cannot be raced on any important track.

The early English Thoroughbred was a bit over 14 hands but the modern American Thoroughbred averages nearly 16 hands, weighs 950 to 1150 pounds in racing condition and adds another 300 pounds after retiring to stud. In looks he possesses a refinement of body and head which shows his Arab ancestry. His withers are pronounced, back rather long, and there is great depth through the girth line to make room for the large heart and lungs needed for running. His head is alert, eyes wide-set, nostrils prominent, profile straight, sometimes a slight Roman nose, as in Man O' War, who had the tough-willed temperament which goes with it. His legs are straight, with dense bone and cable-like tendons. In top racing condition a Thoroughbred carries not an ounce of fat or loose flesh, his coat glistens, his eyes sparkle and veins show prominently over his long flat muscles.

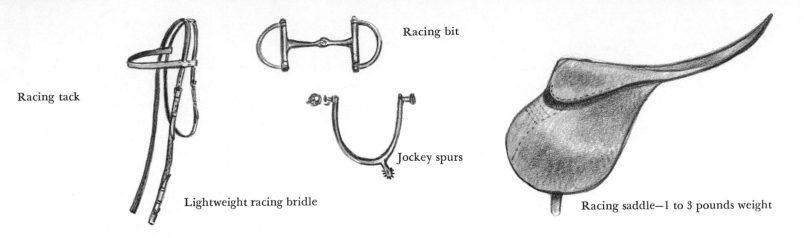

Racing tack

Racing bit

Jockey spurs

Lightweight racing bridle

Racing saddle—1 to 3 pounds weight

According to Cornell University scientists, there is a difference between Thoroughbred blood and that of other horses. They found it has a higher red-cell count, providing a greater quantity of oxygen-carrying hemoglobin. This may account for his ability to outrun all other breeds of horses. Also, any track vet will tell you that the hard-running Thoroughbred has a consistently better blood count than the ordinary nag. This may be partly hereditary but more likely due to the fine care and training which enables him to perform closer to his potential.

Thoroughbreds come in seven colors. About 90 percent are bay, chestnut or brown and 10 percent are black, gray, roan or dun. Some foals appear to be black when born but turn out to be gray. Carry Back, the great race horse, is brown but the average person would swear he was black.

There are approximately 30,000 Thoroughbreds in training today and another 25,000 on some 1,900 breeding farms throughout the country. These farms vary from the one- and two-mare size on up to the huge stud farms in Kentucky, Virginia and California. Some ninety tracks are spotted across twenty-four states and they make horse racing the largest spectator sport in the United States. More than thirty-five million people attend annually and wager over $2½ billion. In all, the Thoroughbred racing industry provides an annual payroll of $250 million to more than fifty thousand people. It is also one of the few sports which polices itself effectively. Through the Jockey Club, the Thoroughbred Racing Association and its Protective Bureau of former FBI men, horse racing has successfully kept out racketeers and other undesirable elements which could easily have ruined it.

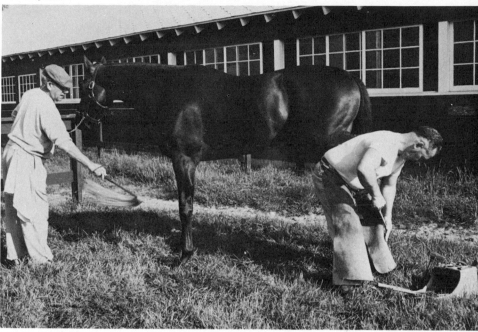

A thoroughbred gets a new set of racing shoes.

More than $88 million is distributed annually in purses, but before you run out and buy a race horse (which can be done quite easily in a claims race), consider the fact that it costs $300 to $400 a month to keep a horse stabled and racing, plus such extras as nomination and starting fees, jockey fees, travel and veterinary care.

Fresh from a win—note lively expression of typical thoroughbred racer.

Many stallions are owned by syndicates these days. A group of breeders get together and share the cost of purchase and maintenance, and also share the stud rights. Recently the first broodmare was syndicated. Bought for $137,000, Honey's Gem once broke the world filly record for the mile, 1:34, and at the time of her purchase was in foal to Swaps, world record-holder for the mile, 1:33 1/5.

There are six different kinds of races: Handicap, Allowance, Claiming, Maiden, Stakes and Futurity.

In a Handicap each horse carries a weight assigned to him by the racing secretary, who takes into consideration the ability of each horse and tries to even things up by adding extra poundage to the better ones. If a jockey and his saddle weigh in at 112 and the assigned weight is 120, then he will have to carry eight pounds of lead in special pockets under the saddle. Top weight is about 130 pounds. The reason Man O' War was raced only as a two- and three-year-old was that the weight got so heavy on him his owner feared it would ruin the horse's legs, so he was retired. Nevertheless he broke two world records, the 1⅜ and 1⅝ miles in 1920. The former still stands. Swaps, carrying maximum weight, broke three world records in 1956—it can be done.

The Allowance race is similar to the Handicap except that the racing secretary at each track fixes a base weight. The better horses carry more than this, the poorer ones less.

In a Claiming race, backbone of most track programs, the racing secretary decides upon a certain figure ranging from $1,500 to $20,000. Any horse can be entered, but the owner must be prepared to sell him for the amount of the claim any time up until the race begins. Horses change hands very often through Claiming races, and some good ones have been picked up cheaply. Stymie was bought for $1,500 and went on to win $918,485. Owners are always trying to think up ways to keep their horses from being claimed. The latest method is to put wads of cotton under the leg bindings so the horse appears to have splints and spavines, the bugaboo of racers.

Maiden races are for horses who have never won a race. These unfortunates are called maidens regardless of sex, but somebody has to win.

The Stakes race is the big attraction both to the betting public and to the racing owners. Here is where the really great horses and jockeys compete. Purses run up to $100,000 or more. The entry fee can be $7,500 or over. Basically, all the horses carry the same weight, except for sex allowances and handicaps for winning a previous big race.

A Futurity is a breeders' race and the richest race in the world. Before the foal is born the owner must nominate it. After it is born the owner begins to pay forfeits at various times until the big race, generally for two-year-olds. If the horse doesn't "have it," the owner drops payments; if the horse shows great promise, then the payments continue at an ever-increasing rate. But there is a pot of gold at the end of the rainbow. The Arlington-Washington Park Futurity in Chicago in 1961 ended up with $357,250 in the kitty—the world's richest purse.

The Triple Crown, dream of every breeder and racing owner, consists of a series of three races, the Kentucky Derby, the Preakness and the Belmont Stakes, open only to three-year-olds. To gain the crown a horse must win all three races. Besides fame and a quarter of a million dollars, a Triple Crown winner becomes enormously valuable at stud. Only eight horses have turned the trick: Sir Barton, 1919; Gallant Fox, 1930; Omaha (a son of Gallant Fox), 1935; War Admiral, 1937; Whirlaway, 1941; Count Fleet, 1943; Assault, 1946, and Citation, 1948.

Training race horses is an exciting but heartbreaking profession. So much time and energy go into preparing for a big stakes race, and one little flaw or accident or tough break along the line can ruin everything.

To start at the beginning, the owner of a Thoroughbred mare must select a suitable stallion from the 2000 or so available. Stud fees range from $150 to $10,000 for a horse like Nashua, 1955 champ. The mare's contribution must be considered, for it has been proved a thousand times over that breeding a poor mare to a great stallion is a waste of time. After the breeding has

Portrait of a champion—Kelso

29

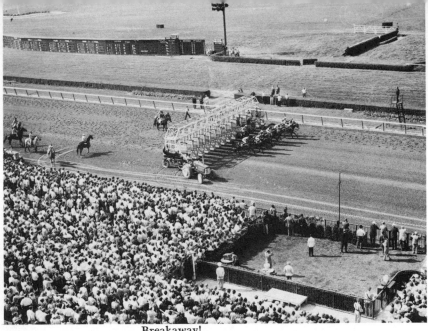

Breakaway!

taken place, chances of the mare's settling (becoming pregnant) are only 60 percent—odds are tough to start with.

Say you pay a $500 stud fee and a foal is born. It will usually be worth a little more than the stud fee, a lot more if a half-brother happens to have won a big race as yours becomes a yearling, a lot less if it turns out to be gawky and ugly.

Human contact is important from the moment the foal is born, in late winter or early spring. The owner will make a point of talking to and petting the wobbly youngster, slip a tiny halter on and off until he is weaned at six months.

Once he passes January 1 of the following year he becomes a yearling and his life is crowded with basic training—none of the old-fashioned western methods of bronco-busting to make a horse manageable in a couple of days. Over a period of two to three months he is taught to take the bridle and bit, the saddle, and to lead. He is always in the company of other colts and fillies his own age, for young horses are less afraid and learn more quickly when they are together. Finally the jockey mounts him, walks him about the track and jogs him a little.

As summer approaches, the owner has a choice of selling him as a yearling or holding on and racing him himself. If it is a large breeding farm and the horse shows a spark of "the right looks," he will be kept, otherwise no. Many breeders make a business of selling all their yearlings and going only this far, but even the one-horse breeder may keep his snappy colt, for dreams run rampant in the hearts of race-horse breeders. This may be the BIG ONE.

Held or sold, the yearling goes to a professional trainer and the serious work begins. The young horse must practice over and over breaking from the starting gate. He must be conditioned every day, warmed up, sprinted, jogged, sprinted, jogged, run hard, clocked, jogged, cooled off, walked. Each day a little faster, a little harder, a little longer. He is run with an older horse to gain confidence. Sometimes the older horse boxes him against the rail. He learns to go out and around. Other times the older horse passes him and the jockey applies the whip. All horses are different. Some will respond to the whip and thrust ahead, others will slow down. A few will stop dead.

All kinds of systems are used. For example, the trainer may order the older horse held back so the young horse is always ahead. As the older horse challenges, the youngster pours it on to stay ahead. Day after day of this and he becomes what the trade calls a front runner. He hates to be passed, will fight to stay ahead. This sounds great and it may win some races. But what happens in a big stakes race like the Kentucky Derby is that a farm with plenty of money will enter two horses. The jockey on the first horse has orders to set a torrid pace so the front runners who don't like to be headed will wear themselves out and be finished at the three-quarter pole. Then on come the horses who have paced themselves and have plenty left for a stretch drive.

There are many tricks to the trade. The owner, trainer and jockey must know them all. A trainer always watches how his horse runs the final quarter. In cheap company it may be three or four seconds behind the first quarter. In good horses it is the same or better. Silky Sullivan, great come-from-behinder a few years ago, ran his final quarters in considerably less time than his first.

Great controversies whirl in the race horse world as to when a horse should actually begin racing. In the early days, the English Thoroughbred was never ridden until a three-year-old, never raced until five, and was in his prime when eight or nine years of age. In the United States today there are almost no Thoroughbreds racing at nine. They are retired for breeding or because they are burned out. Their legs as two-year-olds take too much of a beating to hold up. Even firing, blistering and standing in tubs of ice water for hours at a time doesn't solve the problem. The answer seems to be that they are just raced too young but the demands of a $3-billion industry are hardly liable to permit change.

Most race horses are hot-headed. Many have had some "loose screws" and still been great. A horse named Carefree won sixty-seven races, mostly for one owner who kept selling him only to get him back again. Carefree was completely unpredictable. He might duck through a gap or stop and observe the surroundings. Several times while coming down the homestretch he dashed for the outside fence. Once he jumped it and still got back on the track to win by two lengths. Another day he had a fifteen-length lead when he stopped dead on the homestretch, turned and faced the oncoming field. If his jockey used the whip or urged him on, he'd stop in his tracks. When pulled down he would run his fastest. Such horses give not only the crowd but the trainer heart palpitations.

Over the water at Belmont Park

Head of stretch turn with the winner leading

Only once in an era does a Man O' War come along. "Big Red," as the world called him, was a large horse with near-perfect conformation and lost only one race in twenty-two, and that on a bad start. A clever jockey on a horse named Upset noticed that Man O' War was turned sideways as they prepared to start. He hollered "Let's go!" to a green starter who sent them off, leaving Big Red at the post. Upset beat him by a neck. Man O' War had it all—blinding speed, stamina, weight-carry-ing ability and heart. He just wouldn't allow himself to be beaten. His wins were always big—four, six, ten, even twenty lengths. In his first race he started so fast that his jockey almost fell off. As world records began to fall to him he became the idol of every horse lover in the land. People turned out by the tens of thousands to see Big Red mow 'em down. Odds on him are still the lowest in history: 1 to 100 at Belmont Park (New York). That means a two-dollar bet on the nose (to win) returned two dollars and two cents, *including the bettor's two dollars.* After retiring he became one of the greatest sires of all time and lived to be nearly thirty-one. Two thousand people attended his funeral ceremony, which was accorded military honors by the U.S. First Cavalry Division, which had previously made him an Honorary Colonel.

Saratoga (New York) is the oldest track in the country, opened in 1863. It is famous today not only for its social-register racing and yearling sales which attract buyers from all over the country, but also for its National Museum of Racing, full of the colorful history of horse racing plus some of the finest Thoroughbred art works in existence. Well worth a visit if you're ever in the vicinity.

Hialeah (Florida), one of our most beautiful tracks, is a bird sanctuary. Hollywood, California, has the richest purses. Delaware Park (Delaware) is the hangout for fillies and mares, sponsors of the Distaff Big Three, a trio of championship races climaxed by the $150,000 Delaware Handicap, richest race in the world for female horses. Fillies and mares have a five-pound weight allowance when running against colts and stallions, but the latter still dominate.

Turf Paradise in Phoenix, Arizona, boasts fireproof stalls, a plush clubhouse, private landing strip, is the favorite meeting place for Hollywood bettors, and calls itself "The Home of World Records" because four have been set there. Through the years, however, Belmont Park and Santa Anita (California) have been the scenes of most record-breaking because the big horses go there.

The Keeneland track near Lexington, Kentucky, is one of the few nonprofit ones we have. It is also the focal point for Thoroughbred activity throughout the year—summer yearling sale, fall yearling sale, breeding stock sale in October, horses-in-training sale spring and fall. Over ten thousand horses pass through Keeneland each year.

It was at Keeneland that the new Atlas of the racing world, Rex Ellsworth, made his start. In 1934 he and his brother, both cowhands with big dreams of Thoroughbred racers, rattled into Lexington in a battered truck and asked directions to the Keeneland fall sale. The two brothers had saved $1,000 while working on their father's Arizona ranch. Everything was cheaper in those depression days, and a week later they headed home with six elderly broodmares and two weanlings on their creaking truck. One of the mares carried a foal which eventually won $19,000 for Rex Ellsworth. He stuck with racing and twelve years later, just after World War II, went horse hunting in Europe. From its shambles he brought back a group which included a three-year-old named *Khaled. *Khaled sired the great Swaps and more than two hundred other winners of some 1300 races and over $7 million. Today Ellsworth's 440-acre ranch in Cheno, California, houses one hundred broodmares, and in 1962 he cracked the magic

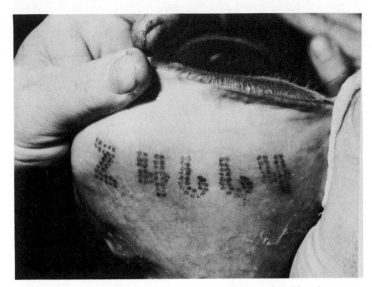

Lip tattoo of racing thoroughbred for positive identification

Willie Shoemaker weighing in

million circle, his horses winning a total of more than $1,200,000 in purses.

The American "tout" (hot tipster), say track officials, is a petty racketeer, the near opposite of his colorful English counterpart. He gives a different horse to each "client" in a race, collects from the winners, who are forever convinced they were "in on a fixed race." Practically no funny business goes on at a track of any size today. The rules are too tight, supervision too relentless, competition too keen.

Racing silks, like Thoroughbreds, originated in England. The first list of 1762 contained seventeen sets of colors. Today the American Jockey Club has nearly three thousand sets of colors which are listed for life and used sometimes three and four generations later by the family. Among the variations of reds are Harvard Crimson, Cyclamen, Flame, Raspberry, Chinese, Flamingo, Indian; blues vary from Teal to Alice, Sky, Flag, Powder, Sea, Yale, Midnight and Cobalt, to name a few. Lines, insignias and geometrical figures are al-

34

lowed on the blouse. One stable hopefully uses a rab-bit's foot.

All trainers like a horse with a hearty appetite. There seems to be validity in the theory that finicky eaters are not good track performers. The average Thoroughbred will put away eight or nine quarts of oats a day plus hay, vitamins and anything else his owner thinks will make him win. Triple Crown winner Assault, who shot to fame and fortune despite poor feet, polished off eleven quarts a day.

The late Grantland Rice, dean of American sports-writers, loved the Daily Double. Highest ever recorded was at Washington Park (Illinois) on August 14, 1939, when the combination of Joy Bet and Merry Caroline returned $10,772.40 for a two-dollar bet. When Granny Rice died, the Thoroughbred Racing Association set up four $10,000 scholarships at Vanderbilt University in Nashville, Tennessee, for high school seniors who wish to follow a career in sportswriting. The scholar-ship, beyond tuition, provides summer employment on a breeding farm, at a race track or on a newspaper.

A Thoroughbred may have perfect conformation and a beautiful way of going but if he is a second or two under racing speed he's useless for the flat track. He may make a fine hack for trail riding and general horse showing or a superb hunter. Or, if he is built right, has great stamina and can jump big, he may very well make a good steeplechaser.

WORLD'S 15 LEADING MONEY-WINNING HORSES

Horse	Starts	1st	2d	3d	Winnings
Round Table	66	43	8	5	$1,749,869
Nashua	30	22	4	1	1,288,565
Citation	45	32	10	2	1,085,760
Swoon's Son	51	30	10	3	970,605
Stymie	131	35	33	28	918,485
Carry Back	37	14	5	7	851,648
Swaps	25	19	2	2	848,900
Sword Dancer	39	15	7	4	829,610
T.V. Lark	55	17	8	6	828,479
Armed	81	41	20	10	817,475
Find	110	22	27	27	803,615
Native Dancer	22	21	1	0	785,240
First Landing	37	19	9	2	779,577
Bold Ruler	33	23	4	2	764,204
Bally Ache	31	16	9	4	758,522

Steeplechasing began in England, where avid horse-men would gather on a Saturday or Sunday and race to a distant church steeple, jumping fences, hedges, stone walls, all at full speed. Gradually courses were set up with various types of colossal jumps involving both height and width. In England today steeplechasing is equally as popular as flat racing, while in Ireland it is the national pastime. In the United States it flourishes mainly on the Eastern seaboard, where heritage and the United Hunts Racing Association, a nonprofit group begun in 1905, have kept it alive. Purses are not as high as those for the flat racers, the average being from $10,000 to $25,000. The $50,000 Temple Gwathmey at Aqueduct is the highest in the country.

Anyone who knows horses and steeplechasing agrees that this is one of the most exciting, exhausting and perilous sports there is. More skill and courage are required of horse and jockey than in any other type of racing—approaching a big jump at full speed, timing the takeoff, avoiding a pileup. No wonder flat-racing jockeys crowd into the infield to watch a steeplechase. They have the deepest respect for their brethren, the jumping jockeys. The pay is lower, the danger is higher. They're allowed to weigh a little more, up to 135 or 140 pounds, but they're great riders.

In a flat race it's a rarity when all the horses don't finish. Not so in a steeplechase. Horses often go down like tenpins. Your heart hangs in your throat. You never know what will happen. Like the time Alligator fell twice in the Maryland Hunt Cup race, was remounted and still won. Or the time Blockade was flying over the Glendale Course in Middleburg, Virginia, with a good lead. Next to the last jump something broke, the saddle twisted and hung loosely under the horse's belly, the jockey grabbed the mane and managed to right himself. Blockade kicked the saddle free and took the last jump with the jockey hanging on bareback, and they won. The ending is not always so happy though. The field

can bunch up, the lead horse fall, and there stands disaster at the head of the line.

The average brush race is 2½ miles, about twice the distance flat racers usually run. Our Grand National at Aqueduct is 3 miles, while the Maryland Hunt Cup race, considered the toughest timber course in the world, is 4 miles, over twenty-two fences. The huge jumps at the Grand National in Aintree, England, including the famous Beaches Brook, a 6-foot brush jump in front of a 16-foot ditch, makes this the most rugged of steeplechase courses. Punchestown is considered one of the best in Ireland, though the country is dotted with them.

Steeplechasers come in various sizes and degrees of attractiveness, but all have a strong, wiry look. Generally they are large, rangy horses with plenty of light under their bellies because of long legs, particularly below the knee and hock. Powerful thighs and gaskins provide the propulsion which jets them over high hurdles and brush jumps with hidden ditches. The impact of landing is so great that heavy leg bones are imperative, especially since 'chasers carry more weight than flat runners (140 pounds average) and land on one front foot as they complete a jump, though the other foot follows immediately.

A good steeplechaser has a wide, intelligent forehead, for quick thinking is an essential part of survival in this rugged business. Scatterbrains are dangerous. Jockeys

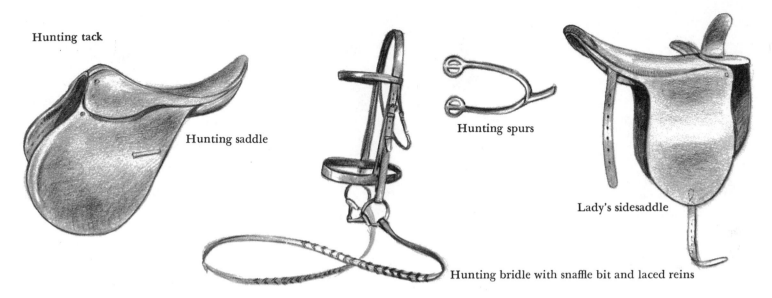

Hunting tack

Hunting saddle

Hunting spurs

Lady's sidesaddle

Hunting bridle with snaffle bit and laced reins

won't ride them. 'Chasers usually have great depth through the girth line, also well-developed shoulders and forearms. They are conditioned right down to nothing but muscle and bone. The jumping part is instinctive. They love it. Still, they must be trained to take all sorts of barriers under every condition. They practice, rain or shine, and under all kinds of lighting conditions, for many a steeplechase has been lost when a horse refused to jump because the sun was in his eyes and he'd never met this condition before.

In the big events, tails are bound tightly so they won't catch going over a brush jump. Cannons are bandaged or strapped for added support. Occasionally a bandage will unravel and a trailing horse will step on it and be thrown. The hazards are endless.

Steeplechase stars are not as well publicized as flat racers, but huntsmen and jumping enthusiasts know them inside and out. Billy Barton was a great one. In the Maryland Hunt Cup race he fell, was remounted, took the last three jumps with the reins all on one side, won and broke the record by 23 seconds. Jolly Roger, Duettiste, Fairmont, Green Cheeze and Bushranger were all outstanding in their time. Battleship, pint-sized son of Man O' War and Quarentine, won the English Grand National against the biggest and best chasers in the world.

Proper hunting attire: *Left:* Master of Foxhounds wears scarlet frock with collar of hunt club colors, black velvet hunt cap, white breeches; hunt boots; carries horn and hunting crop. *Second from left:* Lady member wears formal shad belly hunt coat of black Melton with silk hunting top hat, white stock with gold pin, buff or canary breeches, hunt boots and gloves. *Third from left:* Junior member wears black Melton hunt coat with white stock and hunt cap, buff or canary breeches, informal hunt boots and gloves. *Right:* Gentleman member wears scarlet frock, shad belly or weasel belly with collar of hunt club colors, silk hunting hat, white breeches and hunt boots; may carry sandwich case and hunting flask, also wire cutters.

A brush barrier is dangerous enough, but racing over timber, as in the Maryland Hunt Cup race, is dynamite. Steeplechase horses learn to skim over brush, are perfectly safe if they scrape two or three inches into it, but the timber horse had better clear it cleanly or he and jockey go flying.

Timber jumpers like Brose Hover, Troublemaker and Blockade, another tough little son of Man O' War, deserve the highest credit for bringing real speed and pace to timber racing.

Point-to-point racing has long been popular in Virginia, Pennsylvania, New Jersey, Connecticut and

38

wherever fox hunting is done. A course, marked by flags, is laid out over perhaps five miles of countryside, and the horses jump all types of barriers. Many amateurs excel at this cross-country type of racing.

Jumping jockeys, whether professional or amateur, are a scarred, rugged lot. Silver wire often holds their bones together but the thrill, the challenge, is in their blood just as the courage and heart are in the powerful Thoroughbreds they ride.

For the last two hundred years Thoroughbreds have been used in England, Ireland and America in the noble but expensive affair of pursuing the fox. George Washington, himself an inveterate fox hunter, admitted it to be incurable once it got into your blood. He hunted for hours at a time on his favorite jumper, Blueskin, an iron gray, across the fields of Virginia and Maryland, an area long famous for the sport.

Though people make a ritual of fox hunting, from dress to manners to speech, the horses they ride are practical. A good hunter, regardless of looks or size, must have endurance, a big heart and lots of brains. To provide real pleasure while hunting cross-country, jumping stone walls, post-and-rail fences, brooks, whatever the obstacle encountered in following the baying hounds, the horse must be smooth-gaited, manageable enough to jump at various speeds, willing to leave the crowd, stop dead and stand if necessary.

FOX HUNTING TERMS

Master of Fox Hounds Man or woman in charge of hounds and hunt. His word is law.

Whipper-In Assists the Master in controlling the hounds and hunt. Carries spare set of couples for hounds, wire cutters, spare stirrup leather, flask and sandwiches.

Shad-Belly A coat pattern often worn by members of the hunt.

Hill Topper A rider who follows the hunt from hilltop to hilltop, trying to guess where the kill will take place.

Couples Hounds are counted in pairs because they are coupled together until cast off to start the hunt. A pack of twenty-five hounds is referred to as twelve and a half couples.

Villain Male fox.

Vixen Female fox.

Strike To find and start a fox running.

Tally Ho! The huntsman's cry when the fox is sighted.

Ringer A fox that runs in circles.

Stained Said of scent that is weak or lost when a clever fox runs through cattle or sheep to throw the hounds.

Brush Tail of the fox. The brush together with mask and pads of fox are awarded by the Master to those who arrive at the kill first.

Fox hunting, long popular throughout the eastern part of the United States, has spread to areas of the Midwest and California. Even in the jackpine country of the Rocky Mountain foothills near Denver, Colorado, hunts are held in the traditional manner: gentlemen in pink coats and black bowlers, ladies in black Melton coats, derbies and white stockings. The only difference is that instead of foxes they hunt the wily coyote.

Thoroughbreds, particularly those from Ireland, long ago proved themselves fine hunters. In America many hunters are three-quarters or seven-eighths Thoroughbred, the outcross being to the Cleveland Bay for hunters of weight-carrying ability, or the Saddle Horse for refined ladies' hunters, or the Hackney and Welsh pony for children's-sized hunters.

Fox hunting carries a noble tradition of horses, hounds and people, and here again the Thoroughbred serves the cause most admirably.

5.
The
Standardbred

OF ALL THE BREEDS OF HORSES DEVELOPED IN THIS COUN-
try the Standardbred can most truly be called the People's Horse. Better known as the trotter and pacer, he
sprang from the efforts of little men all over America
who loved good horseflesh and competition. He became a national craze during the 1800's, almost faded
into oblivion when the automobile chased him from
the roads, but has in the last twenty-five years roared
back to popularity at fairs, exhibitions, and especially
as a night racer at lavish arc-lit tracks across the country.

His beginnings? Due to utility, religion and the old
saw that wherever there are two horses you have a horse
race.

41

As roads improved in colonial times, a need arose for a horse that could pull light wagons comfortably around town—the doctor's buckboard, milady's roadster in high style, a delivery wagon. The walk was too slow a gait, the gallop too rough and dangerous. Trotting was more suitable. And what was more fun than a couple of farmers having a little "brush" and trotting wide-open as they headed into town, or the local butcher making the banker eat his dust for half a mile down Main Street on a Saturday afternoon. Sometimes one town challenged another to a trotting match and there were great doings in side bets. The People's Horse worked during the week and trotted in races whenever and wherever the occasion arose.

Flat racing with Quarter Horses and Thoroughbreds was also popular in those early days, but after the American Revolution puritanical New England adapted its Blue Laws, which banned horse racing as irreligious. All tracks were closed by 1802, but trotting meets were allowed to continue. The courts reasoned that racing was a contest to see who could go the fastest. Obviously a trotting horse wasn't going as fast as he could if he were running. Therefore he wasn't racing!

As a result New England became a hotbed for trotters, and its stylish fast-trotting Morgan horses, which originated in Vermont, were the early stars.

Other hot spots sprang up also—Baltimore, Philadelphia, New York. Such was the craze in New York that the city fathers passed an ordinance forbidding trotting faster than five miles an hour except on Third Avenue, which in 1807 was laid out for a trotting speedway as were Jamaica Road in Long Island and later Harlem Lane. "Free-for-All's" were held and anyone with a trotter could come and participate. Each weekend saw a near-mob scene which sent pedestrians scurrying. The real racing of trotters for records or stakes was done under saddle at tracks, the first on Long Island in 1823 when the New York Jockey Club offered a $1,000 prize. By 1840 the high-wheeled sulky and wagon had become the vogue because they produced greater speeds.

Rivaling New England with trotting fever was lower New York State, particularly Orange County, across the Hudson. This area produced the greatest early trotters the world had ever seen, and justly so. For while the Morgans and the Narragansett Pacers and the *Bellfounder line of Boston were flowering winners, *Messenger, a Thoroughbred stallion imported from England in 1788, had already left his hallmark forever upon the trotting world. For twenty years this great colonial stallion stood as a sire in Orange, Dutchess and Westchester counties, in Long Island and northern New Jersey. A descendant of Darley Arabian on his top line (sire), of Godolphin Barb and Byerly Turk on his bottom line (dam), he was as fine a Thoroughbred as ever came to this country. He produced some great running horses in his day and later stars like Gallant Fox, Extermi-

Yearling Standardbreds at pasture

nator, Top Flight, Sea Biscuit, Sun Beau, Man O' War and Whirlaway all carried his blood. But so few were the Thoroughbred mares in *Messenger's time that he was bred mainly to light-harness mares. The offspring had astounding trotting ability and the more they were interbred the greater they became until they absorbed every other line of the trotting family. Thus *Messenger is best remembered as the founding father of the Standardbred, and just about every trotter and pacer living today is descended many times over from this early Thoroughbred stallion.

But old *Messenger's fame might not have reached such heights had it not been for the dream of a hard-headed Dutch-American farmhand, William Rysdyk, to become a horse breeder. Rysdyk lived in Orange County and while working for Jonas Seeley, a trotting-horse trader, he fell hopelessly in love with a colt, born in 1849, whose father was an ugly renegade son of *Messenger, and mother a useless cripple by *Bell-founder (a Norfolk trotter from England) from a *Messenger mare. Bill Rysdyk, an unsentimental man by nature, suddenly began heaping care and affection on this colt. He had to have it. He had to go into the horse business and this little colt would do it, maybe even

43

A pacer

As mares began to be bred to this horse, the results were miraculous—great trotters every one. George Wilkes, the second time he was ever on a track, beat the pride of New England, the famous Black Hawk Morgan, Ethan Allen, in a $5,000 match race in Long Island and went on to become a world champion as did another son, Jay Gould. Six other sons each produced a world-champion trotter, became the glory of the Standard Breed, and wiped out every other male line until the harness horse became literally Hambletonian.

The horse himself produced great trotters during his twenty-six years, the last ten of which Bill Rysdyk charged a preposterous $500 stud fee, highest ever to that time and equal to that of the great flat racer Lexington. In all he produced 1,331 foals before he died in 1875.

The only peculiarity about Hambletonian was that he stood two inches higher at the rump than at the withers. "The trotting pitch," everyone called it, and for years they believed that this was what produced the great length of stride and the immense propulsive power.

Trotters of today seldom have this conformation. The great world-champion Greyhound was four inches taller than he was long, though descended many times over from Hambletonian and consequently from *Messenger. Pacers are generally "downhill all the way," that is, withers slightly higher than rump.

Bill Rysdyk, for gambling on his dreams, became a

make him famous. Seeley finally sold him mother and colt for a $125 promissory note, and Rysdyk struck out on his own. The colt grew into a fine bay stallion, trotted only once against time, beating a local horse all to pieces, and won several prizes at neighboring fairs for his beauty. He had a good even temperament. His body was well muscled, a little on the long side, but with great power and frictionless movements, and he had a mighty stride that literally devoured the ground when he trotted. Rysdyk called him Hambletonian.

44

Trotting Rigs: *Top*—Yesterday. *Bottom*—Today.

rich man, and the horse he loved so much is immortalized in the Hambletonian, greatest of all trotting stakes held for many years at Goshen, New York, heartland of Orange County trotting and home of the Dutch farmhand and his horse. Run at Du Quoin, Illinois, today, it is a mile race for three-year-old trotters, all of whom have been entered before they were born. The purse is often as high as $150,000 and the crowds come from far and near, for the harness horse is still the People's Horse.

There have been many greats among the ranks of harness horses. The first to trot a mile in under three minutes was Yankee, 2:59, at Harlem in 1806.

Record breakers of the 1800's were mostly mares. Lady Suffolk cracked the 2:30 mile. Flora Temple, dainty little speed demon of the 1850's, was the first 2:20 trotter.

A decade later appeared one of the most fantastic trotting mares the world has ever seen. Goldsmith's Maid, a granddaughter of Hambletonian, and described as "beautiful," "spirited," "nervous,"—could not be broken to harness until seven years old. Then the famous trainer-driver Budd Doble got hold of her, straightened her out, and she swept away the opposition. She broke the world's record at fourteen years of age, smashed it a total of seven times, the last at 2:14,

45

and traveled around the country in a private Pullman to perform for hundreds of thousands of people at fairs and exhibitions. This doughty little mare raced until she was twenty, won over $360,000 in days when purses almost never went over $10,000 (an all-time-high money win for harness and flat racers until Sun Beau broke it in 1931), and it was done with sixteen-ounce shoes on each forefoot. Goldsmith's Maid was a national idol, truly a People's Horse.

Maud S., 2:08¾, is remembered as the last of the high-wheeled champions, for as speed became paramount, new innovations were added to help the horse. The kite track with a gentle far turn and long homestretch helped Sonol lower the record. But the great advance came when bicycle wheels were put on the sulky. Records fell quickly for a while, then froze at around 2:04.

On the morning of August 25, 1903, newspapers across the country carried headlines about Lou Dillon trotting a mile in two minutes flat the day before. After a hundred years of trying, the two-minute mile had been reached and all America cheered.

Six years before, a horse named Star Pointer had paced the mile in 1:59¼. It was applauded but pacers were generally considered two to three seconds faster than trotters, which were more popular in those days. Now came the great Dan Patch, who stunned the world by pacing a mile in 1:56¼ in 1903, then 1:55¼ the

next year, and before 93,000 people at the Minnesota State Fair in 1906 hit 1:55 flat, only to have it disallowed. Still, Dan Patch was a legend in his time, having toys, cigars and washing machines named after him.

Meanwhile, Peter Manning lowered the trotting mark to 1:56¾ and the stage was set for the arrival sixteen years later of the most colossal trotter the world has ever seen.

Greyhound, a big gray with a 27-foot stride, brought down the house with a 1:55¼ performance at Lexington, Kentucky, on September 29, 1938. The result of "a cross that shouldn't have been made," Greyhound was gelded and sold for $900 as an ungainly yearling. But once he found his strength and gait he was phenomenal. He won everything in sight and, because there was nothing that could compete against him, retired at the early age of eight, holder of fifteen different world records at all distances from one-quarter mile to two miles, in single and double harness, under saddle and over both major and minor tracks.

It is the likes of Greyhound that keep men breeding horses and wondering if maybe the next colt won't be like him.

Also running at this time was a compact, brawny little pacer named Billy Direct, who proved a whirlwind as a two- and three-year-old, grinding off faster and faster speeds with his string of victories. As a four-year-old he followed the Grand Circuit, and at Lexington a poor starting signal was misinterpreted by his driver Vic Fleming, who pulled the horse up while the others charged on to complete the race. Miffed by the official's mistake, which reflected against the horse's fine winning record, Fleming requested the privilege of starting Billy Direct against time, and in front of the huge crowd the sturdy side-wheeler hacked out history by covering the mile in a torrid 1:55 flat, breaking Dan Patch's thirty-three-year-old record.

There were many who thought this was one record never to be touched, but along came the fabulous Adios family, greatest pacers the world has ever known. First, Adios Harry tied it in 1958, then his half-brother Adios Butler broke it in 1960 with an amazing 1:54⅗, which is today's world pacing record. Beginning in 1950, clocking was done in fifths instead of quarters for greater accuracy.

Results show that the pacer is faster by a second or two than the trotter and this is probably why he now outnumbers the trotter by more than two to one. There are about 11,000 pacers eligible to run in competition and only 5,000 trotters.

Long ago the harness horse established himself as a remarkably strong and durable animal. An American trotter was sent to England in 1829 and covered 100 miles in ten hours and seven minutes, trotting on a five-mile circuit.

The greatest winning horse of all time, harness or

The famous trotter, Su Mac Lad, with Stanley Dancer driving, fights off competition to win the United Nations Trot at Yonkers Raceway.

flat racing, was Single G, a pacer with ninety-eight wins, whose father was twenty-three and mother twenty-two when he was foaled.

The Standardbred goes several miles each day for three or four months to get into racing condition, increasing his speed a mite each week. He swings along easily in a clockwise direction around the track, but the moment he's turned the other way he takes off. That's the direction all races are run and he knows it.

47

ALL-TIME MONEY-WINNING HARNESS HORSES

Trotters	Winnings	Pacers	Winnings
Su Mac Lad	$ 455,499	Bye Bye Byrd	$ 554,257
Darn Safe	450,427	Adios Butler	509,844
Tornese	384,104	Widower Creed	401,056
Trader Horn	370,802	Speedy Pick	366,265
Lord Steward	338,831	Bell Action	353,062
Pronto Don	332,363	Adios Harry	345,433
Scott Frost	310,685	Diamond Hal	334,971
Galophone	286,807	Good Time	318,792
Silver Song	264,863	Caduceus	314,162
Proximity	252,930	O'Brien Hanover	286,276

(Note: Goldsmith's Maid is officially listed at $206,462 though Doble certified her complete money winnings as $364,200.)

The Standardbred closely resembles the Thoroughbred in looks and conformation, is a little heavier-boned, more leggy and inclined to have a Roman nose. The neck is a shade thicker but never bowed or chunky. The croup often falls away sharply to the tail because the hind legs are set farther behind than in his close ancestor, the Thoroughbred. Unlike the Throughbred, he is seldom hot-headed and unmanageable but rather docile and friendly until he moves onto the track. Then he is all business and a great competitor.

Both the trot and the pace are two-beat gaits. In the trot the front foot moves in rhythm with the opposite rear foot; in the pace the front and rear foot of the same side move together. Heavy front shoes up to twenty and twenty-four ounces are used to square the gaits when they are not even. This gives higher front-leg action and actually slows down the horse, so he is re-shod before a race.

The Standardbred averages 15½ to 16 hands in height, weighs 900 to 1300 pounds in racing condition, comes mainly in bay, brown and chestnut and occasionally in roan, gray or black. Most are solid color without even a white star on their face, although sometimes a white sock appears. He is more hearty than the Thoroughbred, less subject to illness and breakdown.

A good harness horse will go as fast or faster in the final quarter of a mile than he did in the first. For example, the quarters may break down into 31; 32; 32; 30, for a total of 2:05, which is better than average time.

Since the beginning of harness racing few world records have been established under actual competition because there are so many bottlenecks, like being boxed in or forced to the outside, which consume time. When an outstanding horse shoots for a record the procedure is to give him the whole track with only another horse or two going along as prompters.

A harness horse, if he breaks gait and moves into a gallop, must be pulled up. If he improves his position by the break he is disqualified. If he breaks going over the finish line and a horse is within a length of him,

Walking out "sweats"

he is penalized or disqualified. Pacers are effectively kept from breaking by a leg harness, called a hopple, invented in 1885 by a railroad conductor who owned a pacer that broke continually.

The word "brush" is used constantly in harness racing. It refers to the spurt, or burst of speed, which a trotter and pacer use to pass or gain the lead in a race. Not every horse has this supergear and none can maintain it for more than a few seconds. But it is the invaluable weapon of a good horse and the driver must know just when to ask for it.

Driving is one of the fascinating aspects of harness racing. Unlike jockeys, the driver can be of any weight since he rides a sulky which is pulled. Some drivers are downright chubby, but this seems to have little or no effect on the horse's winning. Much more important is the driver's skill at maneuvering. The sulky has considerable width and he must sneak through openings with courage and care. If he cuts the field off, he's disqualified.

At the start of a race everyone fights for the rail. If, at the halfway mark, the second horse pulls out to pass the first, he had better succeed because the third horse immediately pulls up to take his position, and if he has to fall back he's locked out. On a turn, this is deadly because the outside horse has considerably farther to go. Or on the homestretch he can be boxed in against the rail, in which case he can only sit there and take it. Good driving is a combination of skill, luck, timing and knowing your horse.

Because weight does not enter appreciably into it, many amateurs train and drive their own horses. In fact, a good 50 to 60 percent of the harness horses in competition are handled by fervid amateurs and two- or three-horse stables. They run at the more-than-three hundred fairs that saturate the country, particularly in the Midwest. It's an exciting sport for the little guy, not nearly so expensive as Thoroughbred racing nor so tightly organized. He can participate in it directly himself. And plenty of amateurs have come up with a standout horse and gained entrance to the big-time world of the raceways.

Essentially there are two worlds in harness racing, that of fairs and exhibitions and that of the raceways. At the raceways the professionals battle for big money with top horses. Parimutuel betting under the lights at night draws tens of thousands of city people. It is here that harness racing has had its phenomenal growth. In 1940 New York State had seventy licensed days in four associations with betting amounting to

A fighting finish between two pacers

$1,703,000; in 1962 the state had 721 licensed days in nine associations with a total betting of $530,000,000.

At the raceways the Free-for-All is the big stakes in that it attracts the fastest horses. Trotters and pacers are not handicapped by weight as in Thoroughbred racing, rather they are classified by time and ability. Claiming races were started only in recent years.

Besides racing, the Standardbred trotter is used at horse shows in light harness classes. He has to pull a four-wheeled roadster with elegant style and display perfect manners and conformation. The horse must

50

Unloading a trotter at race track

show smoothness and high action in the slow trot, also in the Park, or brisk trot. Often race-track horses perform successfully in the show ring, but generally these road horses are selected as yearlings and trained especially for this work.

There are many rags-to-riches stories in the race-horse world. One of the most interesting ones about harness horses concerns two stallions, Axtell and Allerton, who made C. W. Williams "The Napoleon of Independence, Iowa." Williams was born in Chatham, New York, in 1856 and moved West when his father, a retired sea captain, decided to take Horace Greeley's advice. A tall, brawny youngster, Williams used both his head and his hands when he went at a thing, was quick at figures, saved his money and had the knack of working at several jobs at the same time. By night he was an operator in the train yards in Independence, Iowa; by day he ran a successful butter-and-egg business.

From childhood he loved horses, and during the long nights at the railroad yards he pored over trotting magazines and made a concentrated study of bloodlines. One night he saw advertised a semidispersal sale of a trotting farm about fifty miles away. Actually the farm was cleaning out some odds and ends of horses and Williams ended up buying three mares and a gelding for $600. One mare he sold at a profit, the gelding he put on his butter-and-egg route and the other two, Gussie Wilkes, a permanently crippled but well-bred

51

PHOTO FOR WIN
BY JONES PRECISION PHOTO FINISH

YONKERS RCY   YONKERS RCY

How close can you get! Trotters crossing the finish line

mare which cost him seventy-five dollars, and Lou, a half-Standard mare, he decided to breed.

The townspeople thought he was a little daft to pay $600 for four horses, none of which amounted to a hill of beans, and they were sure he'd lost his mind when he shipped the two mares all the way to Lexington, Kentucky, to breed. John Hussey, who worked for Williams in his creamery, his butter-and-egg business, on his small farm and in his trotting venture, went with the mares while Williams stayed home to switch trains by night and keep his diminutive empire going around the clock.

Naturally Hussey's instructions were to breed to the best blood possible. But Williams couldn't afford to pay a high stud fee and Hussey quickly discovered that none of the owners of top stallions in Lexington were falling over backwards to breed to a couple of mares from Iowa, a non-Standard and a cripple.

But Hussey was persistent and eventually found two horses which he considered suitable. One was Jay Bird, a son of the famous George Wilkes, but roan, a color which most trotting men wouldn't be caught dead with, and on top of that he was going blind! The other stallion was William L, described by Hussey as splendidly gaited, very fast and one of the handsomest colts in Kentucky, except for the fact that he had crooked hind legs and one very bad hock! If ever a bunch of sorry horses were mated, this was it.

Left: Show roadster for light harness showing *Right:* Sulky for racing

Two foals arrived in due time, both colts, and Williams named them Axtell and Allerton.

Axtell, whom Williams trained and drove himself without any previous knowledge or experience, was undefeated as a two-year-old and lowered the record for two-year-old stallions from 2:26 to 2:23. As a three-year-old he again won every race and smashed the world record for that age from 2:18 to 2:15½ to 2:14¾ to 2:14 to 2:12. This last speed also broke the all-age stallion record and that evening Williams sold the colt for $105,000, at that time "the highest price ever paid for a horse of any age, breed, sex or gait, anywhere in the world, ancient or modern, American or foreign."

Williams sold the colt because he said he had a better one at home. People laughed, but out came Allerton as a five-year-old and lowered Axtell's world stallion record to 2:10, then to 2:09¼, and Williams refused $150,000 cash for him.

Allerton never proved a great sire, although he did number among the ancestors of pacing champion Billy Direct. Axtell, however, went on to become an outstanding stud, his son Axworthy being one of the great progenitors of modern harness racers.

Luck you say? Of course it was. But not entirely so. Little guys have always loved the harness horse. They kept the breed alive in its lean years and they'll do it again. That's why when those big pacers or trotters come winding down the stretch at a raceway, state fair, or a half-mile country track, you can be sure you're seeing the People's Horse from stem to stern.

53

6.
The
Quarter Horse

A SHORT, CHUNKY HORSE WITH A BARREL CHEST AND muscles like a wrestler is sweeping the country on a tidal wave of popularity never before seen in the horse world. If you'd asked an Eastern stable owner ten years ago what a Quarter Horse was he'd have said, "That's only a Western fad." But if he puts on a horse show this year, chances are that half the program or more will be devoted to Western classes, and that means the Quarter Horse. Thanks to this sleek, gentle hunk of brawn we now have such oddities as Connecticut cowboys and Virginia cowgirls as well as barrel racing at the National Horse Show in New York City.

Since World War II a whole new world of Western

riding has grown up and the Quarter Horse is at its heart. It began because people had more time and money, and owning a horse was a long-cherished dream that could come true. But they wanted a practical horse that had good looks and sense, no firebrand like the Thoroughbred, but one that could pick up and move if asked to, an easy keeper that could be ridden without a lot of Fancy Dan clothes. A horse that had breeding and that they could be proud of anywhere.

For all this the Quarter Horse filled the bill. He was a tough little fellow with a look of mammoth strength, yet wonderfully good-natured. He could start like a jet, stop on a dime, run a quarter of a mile faster than any other horse known. He was the original American horse, has a most colorful history and in recent times finally earned a pedigree. He had keen intelligence, and when trained in his profession became one of the most highly skilled of all animals.

What was his profession? In the beginning he was the colonial work horse and quarter-mile racer, from whence he gained his name. Later he crossed the country with the frontier, wandering, working and racing with its hardy pioneers. At last he found a home in the Southwest, in its vast cattle country. For the past hundred years he has been and still is the ranch-horse supreme, the cowboy's companion.

The Quarter Horse is no fancy-stepping parade horse. He doesn't make a high-goal polo pony. He is too heav-

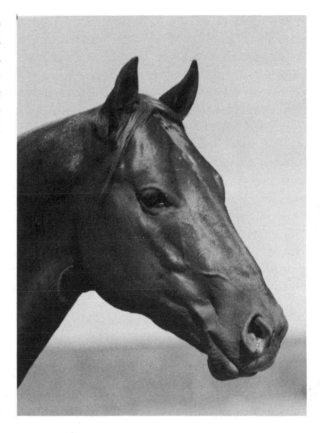

ily muscled and short of stature to compete in the hunting and jumping field. But as a range horse working cattle with speed and dexterity, intelligence and determination, he has long been without a peer. For calf roping, steer wrestling, cutting and reining and barrel racing, all Western competitive events which grew up around the cowboy and his horse, no other breed can match him.

The history of this stubby gallant animal goes back before the Declaration of Independence, to the earliest days of America. Before the white man came, there was not a single horse on the North or South American continent. The Spanish brought the first—Columbus on his second voyage, Cortez for his expeditions against the Aztecs, and Ponce de Leon to Florida in 1513. Horses escaped from all these sources, multiplied and spread into herds that fanned out into Mexico, across the Great Plains, and from Spanish settlements in Florida and Georgia northward into the Carolinas and Virginia.

The Spanish horse was a sturdy little animal, made fast and sure-footed by infusions of Arabian and Barb blood brought to Spain by the Moorish invasion in 718. The most beautiful strain was the Spanish jennet, but all were tough, practical horses capable of surviving on almost nothing. They flourished on the North American continent, became the famous mustang, the Indian pony and the cow pony, and from his blood in both the East and West rose the true Quarter Horse.

When the first colonists moved inland along the coast of Virginia and the Carolinas, the Spanish horses were already running wild there, and it was great sport for the young men of the day to catch and race them. An early diary describes these wild horses as "not very tall but hardy, strong and fleet."

Circular tracks were nonexistent, flat straightaways hard to find, so main streets of towns were used. Contestants paced off 440 yards and made their bets. "At the drop of a hat" they were off! Horse racing was legalized in the colonies around 1625 and that made the "Quarter-of-a-Mile-Running Horse," as he was first called. A practical horse, he pulled a plow or a cart or a wagon during the week, and on Saturday afternoons or whenever a challenge was thrown at him, he raced.

Soon towns were challenging each other. Bets of farms, slaves, even banks, were made, and the best Quarter-Racing horses in Rhode Island, a hotbed of the sport, dueled with the best of Virginia in a famous series of match races. The former won hands down, to the South's chagrin, and afterward owners began carefully selecting studs to improve the breed. The first important outside infusion came in 1752 from *Janus, an English Thoroughbred who, because he had Quarter Horse conformation, was considered a freak and denied registry in the English Stud Book. But in America he helped the racing qualities of the Quarter Horse immensely, while still keeping its chunky conformation.

The Mustang

Until 1800 American enthusiasm in horse racing had centered on races up to a quarter-mile, but then tastes began to follow the British mode of longer distances, one to four miles. By 1830 the Quarter-Racing Horse had lost such popularity that it was almost extinct, although its blood was good enough to assist valuably in founding the American Thoroughbred through thirty-three horses and mares listed in Bruce's Stud Book on Thoroughbreds.

The Quarter Horse continued to be bred and used on the American frontier. Constant infusions of Thoroughbred blood were made to extend the horse's running ability and to keep its conformation from becoming too coarse and musclebound. But such was its decline in popularity that the name "Quarter Horse" was not even used for a time. The animal was strong and tough though, and adapted itself easily to the needs of the settlers moving West, especially to Texas.

While the East was turning to fancy Thoroughbreds for class and long-distance racing, Texas began to utilize the Quarter Horse for ranch work. Here it grew with the land, the history and the lore. Here it carried Davy Crockett to the Alamo and Custer's men to Little Big Horn, transported the Texas Rangers and herded longhorns on the great cattle drives to the railheads in Kansas after the Civil War.

The horse was crossed into the mustang, his distant cousin who had reached the Great Plains through Mexico. A tough, wiry rascal, undersized from short rations and from being inbred, the mustang got his name directly from the Spanish *mesteño,* meaning a horse free to graze and roam though still owned. The Texas ranch horse did everything, and his intelligence and maneuverability around cattle was what made him superior. Horse and man became a team that worked an unforgettable trade.

It must be pointed out that the Quarter Horse was, at its inception, only a type, not a breed: a short, chunky, compact horse, close-coupled, heavily muscled hind legs well set under him for fast turning and quick starts, a smooth gait for all-day riding, an easy keeper with high intelligence and a wonderfully docile temperament. These are the qualities that made him a great range horse throughout the West, capable of doing anything that the frontier required of him.

WHAT IS A QUARTER HORSE . . .

He's half a ton of poised and controlled energy, held on an easy rein and a hair trigger.

He's a workin' man who can earn his keep on the range all week—and be a handsome dandy at the track on Sunday afternoon.

He's proud when he stands; looks lazy when he walks—

But when he runs he can whip the tears from the corner of your eyes and plaster your hat brim against the crown.

He's big in the haunches, supple in the withers, stout in the neck and wide across the chest . . . to hold his great heart.

He's thunder and lightning between your knees and a poem in flight across the pasture.

He's cow-smart and brave--though sometimes a clown—and to the man with sky in his eye and mud on his boot, the Quarter Horse is a faithful hand. . . .

And a friend.

JOHN D. KEMP

To bring speed and quality to the Texas Quarter Horse, several great sires such as Steel Dust, Copper Bottom, Cold Deck, Rondo, Traveler, Peter McCue and Joe Bailey all came from the East, and by 1890 the Quarter Horse, as he is presently known, was established throughout the West.

Cutter Bill—American Quarter Horse champion in typical Quarter Horse pose.

It cannot be denied that the Quarter Horse has been improved, even sustained, by the American Thoroughbred. In fact, there was a long-standing joke among Thoroughbred breeders that a Quarter Horse was "nothing more than a Thoroughbred who had lost his papers," while a fighting-mad Quarter-Horser would shout back that his strain was "guaranteed to carry no Thoroughbred blood." Neither side was right, although the former was nearest. A pedigree check of some of the best Quarter Horses being raced today shows that they are often three-quarters Thoroughbred.

In moving the Quarter Horse from a type to a breed, one of the important elements has been the contribution made by the King's Ranch in Texas. This 823,000-acre spread, unsatisfied with its wrangling horses, decided to create its own breed and chose the Quarter Horse to do it. The results have proved to be a major contribution to the standard and quality of the horse.

But within any breed of animal are families whose greatness is established by one outstanding individual whose merits and abilities and conformation are unsurpassable and who, most important of all, transmits these qualities to his heirs. With the Quarter Horse it has been King (1930–58), permanent registry number P-234. A winner himself, though not on a sensational scale, he had the quality of his name, and his progeny has performed in near miraculous fashion in all types

59

Photo: Quarter Horse Journal

Poco Lena—champion cutting horse and winner of nearly
$100,000 in action.

of events throughout the stock-horse world, winning all the major races, cutting contests, and halter contests for conformation which exist. They, in turn, have been producing get of equal quality, with the result that King's heirs now dominate the breed.

One of his daughters, Squaw H, beat every horse that was ever run at her for ¼ mile. A granddaughter, Poco Lena, is the highest money-winning cutting horse of all time—a few dollars short of $100,000. In recent years it is not unusual to find a vast majority of the top ten cutting horses in the country to be his children or grandchildren.

Surprisingly, King's bloodlines are as near to being all Quarter Horse as they come, an exception rather than the rule, for Thoroughbreds have long dominated because of their racing qualities. King was of Traveler

60

breeding, being a son of Zantanon, the Man O' War of Mexico, who conquered just about everything run against him in Mexico and the southwestern United States. He was a son of Little Joe, one of the truly great Quarter Horse sires of all time, and he in turn was by Traveler, racer and sire supreme of his day.

Such remarkable sires as King come along but once in an era, and theirs is always a major factor in re-vitalizing the breed.

Quarter Horse racing, since early colonial times, has usually been between two contestants. Bets and side bets were made, the two horses with riders lined up, somebody dropped a hat and 440 yards later the winner picked up his money. The poor man's race horse he was often called, but not any more.

In the past decade Quarter Horse racing has grown beyond the imaginations of the few men who started it, or better, restarted it because the sport was about dead. In 1949 William Kyne, then president of the Bay Meadows track in San Mateo, California, decided to try a new twist and use a Quarter Horse stake of 330 to 440 yards each day as the first race. They soon became so popular with racing fans that the California State Fair circuits added two Quarter Horse races a day to their racing cards. The purses were small at first and the horsemen who entered did so only for love of the sport.

The public became excited when two out of three races ended in a photo finish, and dead heats occurred frequently. Everything began to mushroom. Purses bounced up and up, reaching the $10,000 to $20,000 level. The attraction, the challenge and now a whole new world of breeding, training, and racing Quarter Horses has come into being. The colonial Quarter-of-a-Mile-Racing Horse has made the big circle and is back where he started with only his name shortened. Races vary in length from 220, 330, 350 to 400 and 440 yards, occasionally beyond. World record for the $\frac{1}{4}$ mile is 21.8 seconds.

Quarter Horse racing is now recognized in sixteen states and is on a year-around basis, the total purse distribution being nearly $3 million annually. The All-American Futurity for Quarter Horses is run at Ruidoso Downs in New Mexico and is the richest horse race, dollar for distance, in the world. Last year ten horses divided $222,850 after a 400-yard sprint.

Quarter-Racing horses are handicapped according to speed and weight, the best receiving an AAA rating; the next AA; next A. Also, a Register of Merit is given to outstanding performers. A top racing Quarter Horse, if put up for sale, will bring upwards of $50,000, the highest to date being $100,000.

Another important phase of work in which this remarkable horse dominates is the performance class. As stated before, in cutting, roping and reining events the Quarter Horse has no equal. It takes hours, days and months of training up to three years to make a great

61

cutting horse, and the training doesn't begin until he's a three-year-old. This is the area in which intelligence and the desire of the horse to work cattle are most needed.

Quarter Horse owners and enthusiasts annually sponsor at least a thousand shows throughout the United States and Canada, at which more than thirty thousand registered Quarter Horses compete. Classes include several halter divisions where horses are judged on conformation alone, also calf roping, cutting, reining, barrel racing, pole bending, Western pleasure, Western riding and stakes racing. Most of the horses will compete in two or three classes or more.

Two major reasons for the popularity increase of the Quarter Horse are its clinics and youth activities, both of which are giving rise to a new era of knowledgeable horsemen.

Quarter Horse clinics are held all over the country— from Maryland and Connecticut to Ohio and Louisiana and Texas and Washington, on into Canada. At the clinics, college professors, cowhands and judges teach interested adults and children about conformation, breeding, feeding, training, using and enjoying the Quarter Horse.

Also, the American Quarter Horse Association has seen to it that youngsters have their own classes in which to compete. For these they can train their own horses or climb aboard Pop's mount, and the top all-around contestant receives a special trophy.

Tonto Bars Hank, champion racing Quarter Horse and holder of several track and world records

That Quarter Horse raising has become big business can readily be seen by the results of the auctions which take place constantly across the country. They number more than a hundred a year with total receipts close to $7 million and the almost-five thousand horses sold average out to about $1,500 per head. It is nothing for a

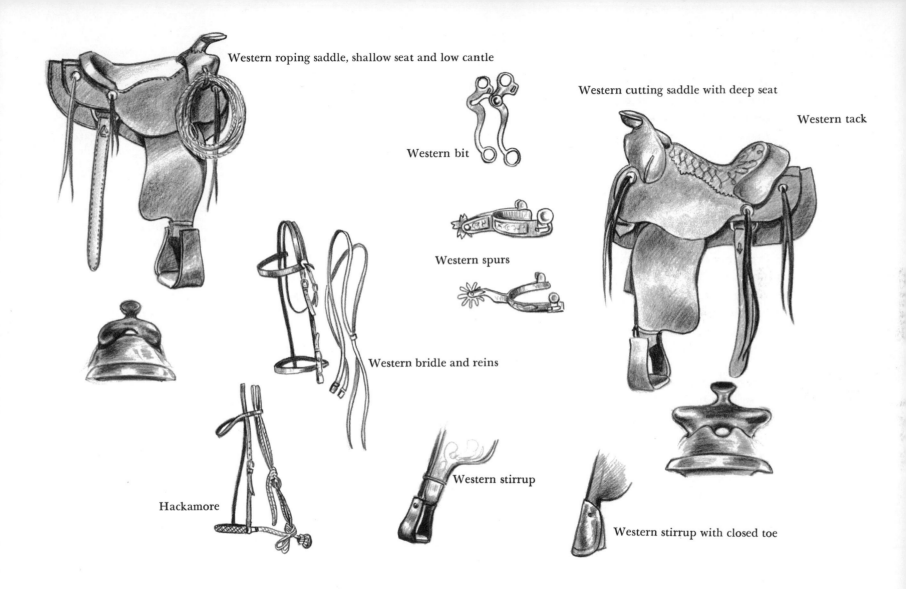

Western roping saddle, shallow seat and low cantle

Western bit

Western cutting saddle with deep seat

Western tack

Western spurs

Western bridle and reins

Hackamore

Western stirrup

Western stirrup with closed toe

well-bred mare that is a proved producer to bring from $10,000 to $30,000, and top stallion prospects command handsome prices also.

From eighty to a hundred Quarter Horses are annually awarded the title of Champion. This much-sought-after accolade comes only after a horse has garnered sufficient points in both conformation and performance classes. Thus a good-looking Quarter Horse that can do nothing never receives the title, neither does the ugly duckling who is a great performer.

Probably the single most important factor which has brought the Quarter Horse out of a type into a breed has been the American Quarter Horse Association, begun in 1941 and now boasting a membership of more than twenty-five thousand. It is one of the youngest of all horse-breeders' groups and one of the most efficient.

From its beginning the organization set about to register all Quarter Horses by the end of twenty years, that is, all Quarter Horses which met the standards of the breed. To do this, every animal, before being permanently registered, was first looked over by inspectors to make certain it was true to the type and quality previously agreed upon. This entailed endless work, but the result is that the Quarter Horse of today is the most uniform of any horse breed existing, not perfect, but nevertheless of high quality considering the variegated past of the breed.

The registration books were closed as of January 1, 1962. This means that only the offspring of those now recorded can be registered and called Quarter Horses with more outcrossing for conformation or racing speed. The Quarter Horse is officially a breed, and as the years roll by he will become more firmly standardized and perfected.

Some people argue that the books were closed too soon, others that they weren't closed soon enough. Time alone will tell. Regardless of the outcome, the Quarter Horse, descendant of Columbus's Spanish horse and colonial America's race horse, with some mustang and cow pony and a lot of Thoroughbred stirred in, and product of the melting pot which is America, will go on doing his multifold job on ranches and in Western competition wherever he is, doing it with all the grit and spunk of his proud heritage.

7.

The Morgan

ONE OF THE GREATEST HORSES AMERICA HAS EVER PRO-
duced was a jaunty little bay stallion foaled about 1789
called Justin Morgan. Strong of heart and princely in
carriage, this amazing animal was only 14 hands, or
pony size by current standards, yet because of his deep,
wide chest, heavily muscled loins, legs and guts of iron,
he outworked, outran, outtrotted, outpulled and out-
acted just about every horse in his native Vermont.

The story of this horse is as much a legend as fact,
for his first owner Justin Morgan, the only person who
might have substantiated his breeding and after whom
he was named, died before the horse grew famous. All
the research by scholars and horse lovers since then has
only compounded the confusion.

It seems that Morgan the man was a part-time school-teacher, tavern manager and horse breeder in West Springfield, Massachusetts, honest but always poor. Because of bad health he moved his family to what is now Randolph Center, Vermont, in 1788. In 1791 he returned to West Springfield to collect an old debt and, apparently unable to obtain cash, took a three-year-old gelding and a two-year-old colt as payment. Back home he disposed of the older horse, but the colt is said to have been too small to be saleable. Or perhaps Morgan loved his little bay stallion too much to sell because he broke him completely as a saddle horse. Even after his wife died and his five children were given to friends to care for, Justin Morgan held on to his horse, trying to make a meager living by breeding him wherever he could. He advertised the little bay stallion as his "Dutch horse, Figure," an animal of "beauty, strength and activity." Nothing was mentioned of his breeding except that "Figure sprang from a curious horse owned by Colonel De Lancey of New York, but the greatest recommendation I can give him is, he is exceedingly sure of foot and gets curious colts." ("Curious" in that day meant rare or fine.)

The horse has been described as about 14 hands and weighing around 950 pounds, a clear dark bay without a white hair on him. He had the look of a blooded horse, fine head, small ears set well apart and carried alertly, large expressive eyes and refined muzzle that

66

Morgan show buggy

we now associate with the Arabian, but his head was not as short nor as dished.

His body and carriage were what attracted people. His powerful neck with its high-arched crest was set on a deep chest and short barrel. He was compact and built like a bulldozer, but without a hint of coarseness. What made him low were very short cannon bones and exceptionally heavy muscling of forearms and gaskins. His feet were neat and clean and his head was always held high and arched proudly, a characteristic of every Morgan. The only objection to him was lack of size, but this he made up for with courage and strength. When he was in light harness or under saddle, his movements rang with class and springy action.

Justin Morgan was obviously proud of his horse, but he lost him on debts shortly before dying in 1789.

Northern New England was a hard land at that time. A beautiful horse that couldn't work was useless, and his subsequent owners put him to work. He cleared land and hauled logs, also won "pulling bees," short running races and trotting races, for bets of rum and silver. At the age of fifteen he was entered in a drawing match that took place at General Butler's tavern in St. Johnsbury. Many of the opponents were large draft horses, yet he beat them all.

The horse was bought, sold, traded, acquired in lieu of bad debts by more than fourteen different owners. The game little stallion always had to work his heart

67

out. When he was nineteen years old he hauled freight as part of a six-horse team. Even in his late years he is described as being remarkably youthful in appearance. Age never quenched his spirit. Hard work, even abuse, never sapped his vigor. His legs remained sound to the end. At thirty-one, when he had earned the right to a clean, dry stall, he stood in an open yard in a roaring Vermont winter competing with other horses for what little feed there was. He died from the result of a kick in 1821. Never in history has a horse had to earn every oat and accolade as hard as this one did.

After his death it was noted that his sons and daughters produced horses of the same type—the thick, powerful body, the highly arched crest, the proud head with small spike ears, the naturally high tail, the short back and the highly animated movements yet wonderfully docile temperament. Usually bay in color, they began to be called Morgans, and soon there was great demand for them as light harness horses and saddle horses in Boston, New York and Philadelphia. Morgan blood became the vogue in trotters and New England horse breeders reaped a fortune. No one had ever checked the lineage of the little bay stallion, although horse traders made wild claims.

Then in 1841 a George Bernard claimed in a sworn affidavit that the original Justin Morgan came from Canada. This started a controversy that rages to this day. Some insisted the horse to be of early Dutch blood;

others that he came from Hartford Thoroughbreds. The generally accepted lineage claims his father to be True Briton, a horse raised and owned by James De Lancey, "father of the New York turf," from English Thoroughbreds he had imported to New York to race. When the American Revolution broke out, De Lancey, a Tory, went back to England and gave True Briton to

Set of Sire Class at Morgan National Horse Show. Sire is at
extreme left; the others are his sons and daughters.

his young cousin, Colonel James De Lancey, a brilliant rider who fought with the British forces occupying New York and Long Island. The horse gained fame for its beauty and speed. One day while Colonel De Lancey visited his mother in the Bronx, three colonial soldiers stole the horse out of spite and sold it secretly in Hartford. After the revolution and amnesty, Justin Morgan leased the horse for breeding purposes while in West Springfield.

True Briton or Beautiful Bay or Traveler, as the horse was known at various times, traces back in direct male line to the Byerley Turk and on his dam's side to the Godolphin Arabian. Thus True Briton was of strong Arabian blood and came from the very foundations of the English Thoroughbred. The dam of Justin Morgan is generally considered to be by Diamond, again a De Lancey horse tracing back to *Wildair, one of the most famous horses in America at the time and a grandson of the Godolphin Arabian.

Justin Morgan was thus a high percentage of Arabian blood, and it shows even today in the finely chiseled heads and proud carriage. Also, many Morgans, like many Arabians, have one less vertebra than the average horse, thus accounting for the shortness of back.

There have been other great horses in history, but few if any have transmitted their quality with such phenomenal success as did Justin Morgan. The horses which he fathered were so stamped with his image that even after several generations and admixtures of foreign blood, the family likeness was so striking they could be spotted immediately. Nor has a single horse ever added so much to so many breeds.

Justin Morgan, through his grandson Black Hawk, and great-grandson Ethan Allen, two of the fastest trotters of their day, profoundly influenced the trotting world in the 1850's. Eventually the blood was absorbed into the development of today's Standardbred to the extent that Greyhound has five crosses, and Titan Hanover, the first two-minute two-year-old in history, has twenty-two crosses back to this famous colonial stallion.

Justin Morgan's descendants were basic also in developing the American Saddle Horse in Kentucky, Tennessee and Missouri, giving these three- and five-gaited animals much of their beauty, animation and stamina.

Later, Morgan blood helped establish the Tennessee Walking Horse, whose popularity is sweeping the South today. The Standardbred stallion, Allan 7623, originator of the breed, had as his dam a Morgan mare who was granddaughter of the famous Black Hawk.

Girl winning Model Filly Foal Class

In the West he helped found the beautiful California Palomino parade horse and has for years been used successfully as a stock horse as many an old-time cowboy will verify. Morgan blood has upgraded almost every breed of horse we have. When crossed with the Arabian,

A playful Morgan

Riding a Morgan bareback

he has produced the flashy Morab. Crosses to the Welsh pony produce an ideal children's horse.

The Morgan survives today as the best all-purpose horse we have. Registered Morgans have made a stirring comeback since their decline around 1900. Their popularity has now spread to the Midwest and Far West, with All-Morgan shows springing up strongly in these areas. And a Morgan Horse Show is a sight to see. It includes everything from Model, or halter, classes to Roadster and equitation classes, jumping and old-time "pulling bees" as part of the special Justin Morgan Class. Owners of Morgans really enjoy their horses in the multitude of ways they can be used. Because of their easy gait they make great trail riders and due to their flashy movements are natural parade horses. Not infrequently they appear in Western cutting and roping classes, for the Morgan is a neat, handy horse that will do a stout job anywhere.

The strength of the Morgan still lies in the northeastern United States. The National Morgan Horse Show is held annually at Springfield, Massachusetts, and horses come from all over the country to compete. Were old Justin to come back and see his thousands of descendants engaged in the many classes that make up the Morgan National, he would certainly puff up with pride, for they have the same smooth-riding qualities, beauty, snappy action and strength that their illustrious forebear bequeathed them.

Morgan head

8.

The American Saddle Horse

IMAGINE A HORSE THAT COMBINES THE ARABIAN'S BEAUTY, the Thoroughbred's size and fiery temperament, the Morgan's sturdiness, the action and racing speed of the trotter and pacer. Add to the dream a bold, commanding presence, brilliant carriage and graceful movement from each highly spirited toss of the head to the crisp precision with which he lifts his feet. There you have the American Saddle Horse, undisputed monarch of the show-horse world.

Each breed of horse exudes one basic quality. With the American Saddler it is splendor, at the awe-inspiring level. Often in a championship the huge crowd will spontaneously begin to cheer a great performance just as one cheers at the end of a concert or stage play.

73

Often called a peacock, the American Saddle Horse is much more like a ballet dancer, moving at different tempos, always with rhythm, grace and precision. Years of training lie behind a great performance, and like the ballet dancer who wears special slippers, heavy make-up, and beautiful costumes to gain the effect, the Saddle Horse uses props to bring out the aesthetic side of his act. It is an exhibition of airy buoyancy, of controlled animation, and when you go away, the memory lingers. You know you have seen splendor.

Yet he is much more than a great show horse—this is only a by-product. Basically he was developed to be ridden and driven, thus his habitually fine gaits make him a pleasure horse par excellence.

Around 1800 the area of Kentucky, Tennessee, and Missouri was dotted with farmers who gloried in good horses. Many fine ones of different breeds had been brought in. The Narragansett Pacer, a classy little speedster from colonial Rhode Island whose comfortable gaits made him an ideal lady's mount, the Canadian pacer who had speed and class, Thoroughbreds, Morgans, trotters, all were there in one form or another. Farmers, though not rich, took the same interest in horses that we take in cars today. They wanted the best. That meant the most beautiful in carriage and action as well as the most comfortable to ride, so they created their own breed. The blood they used came from the same source as the Quarter Horse, the Standardbred,

even the Morgan. The difference lay in selection of the individual. Whenever a horse of extremely fine gaits and conformation was found, farmers brought their best mares to his court.

Such a horse was Tom Hal, a Canadian pacer foaled in 1806, imported from Canada to Philadelphia, where a Dr. Boswell bought him and rode him home to Lexington, Kentucky. How men boasted of their horses in those days! Dr. Boswell rode him from Lexington to Louisville, over eighty miles, from sunrise to sunset, then back to Lexington the next day, all at a pace, just to win a $100 bet. This great old blue roan stallion lived to be forty-one, founded strains of early saddlers in Tennessee, Indiana and Kentucky, and also contributed to the Standardbreds and the Tennessee Walking Horse. One of his great-grandsons sired the mother of Bourbon King, an outstanding Saddle Horse in our time.

By 1840 Kentucky Saddlers were a popular riding and driving breed. They lined the hitching posts in front of courthouses whenever court was in session; they stood between the shafts of carriages before churches on Sunday. Some men boasted of how high their horses stepped at a trot, the smoothness of a canter, so competitions were held at country fairs to see just who had the best-going horses. Thus began the horse show whose demands have helped improve and refine the American Saddle Horse no end.

74

The horse established a reputation during the Civil War when Morgan's cavalry made its famous raid through Indiana and Ohio. Slipping through Northern lines, Morgan, with some two thousand men mounted on Kentucky and Tennessee Saddlers, attacked garrisons and towns and wrought havoc for over three weeks in what amounted to a hit-and-run endurance race, twenty-five-, thirty-five-, forty-mile forced marches with artillery almost daily to escape pursuing Federal troops. Stolen mounts fell by the wayside, but the Saddlers held up to the end.

It was just before the Civil War that the first important injection of Thoroughbred blood occurred. Denmark, a great race horse, was bred to a Saddler known as "the Stevenson Mare," and the result was a horse named Gaines' Denmark, forefather of almost every Saddle Horse living today. Thoroughbred blood helped the Saddler by giving it size and speed without erasing its basic qualities.

Many of the foundation sires of other breeds helped establish the Saddle Horse. *Messenger and *Bellfounder both contributed, as did *Denmark, *Copperbottom, Stump-the-Dealer and others.

Crossing different breeds of horses does not always succeed. The weaknesses often remain while the desirable characteristics are lost. This happened many times to the Saddle Horse, but bloodlines that produced poor horses were abandoned while those that produced good ones were maintained until selective breeding and especially inbreeding finally established the horse to the point where today it has outstanding uniformity of type.

In the 1870's the Saddler became the horse of the man who earned a little more. He was perfectly gaited, practical for riding and/or driving, and supremely beautiful. Naturally his price was higher, but he represented something special, just as a good car does today.

Thus did the Saddle Horse evolve from the utility animal of the man who rode and drove his own horse to the great show horse he is today. And a brilliant animal he is, with a long supple neck, finely chiseled head, ears pricked forward and a short, strong back that supports plenty of weight. His legs have flat, clean joints, and the bone itself is flat, that is, wide from the side but knife-thin from the front. In height he ranges from 15 to 16½ hands. He is usually solid in color, either chestnut, bay, brown, black, gray or occasionally roan. Often he has flashy white leg markings like socks or stockings. Always he is grace and elegance combined with strength.

There are two classes of Saddle Horses—the three-gaited, which has a clipped, or roached, mane and tail, moves at a walk, trot, and canter, and the five-gaited, prince of horses, which carries a full mane and tail, moves at a walk, trot, canter, slow-gait and rack.

The three-gaited Saddle Horse, sometimes called a

moving from his position, a trick which Saddle Horses can often do.

The walk, trot and canter are normal gaits in almost every horse; the slow-gait and rack are not. Very few horses can be taught them. Some Saddle Horses cannot learn them and thus remain three-gaited. The slow-gait can be either an amble, slow pace, stepping pace, running walk or fox-trot according to horse-show rules, though current fashion dictates that it be the stepping pace, a slow, highly animated movement. The rack is a four-beat gait done at racing speed or as fast as the horse can travel without losing form. The steps are taught in many ways, such as urging the young horse out of a walk as he moves downgrade or pulling his front shoes so his feet get a little sore.

Saddle Horses in the show ring carry very long toes and weighted shoes. This tends to increase stride and action as well as balance so that a clean even canter and a collected trot are possible. In a horse of true motion the feet move back and forth in one plane, front and hind equally springy, no dragging, no paddling or dishing in. Here again these faults can be helped, even corrected, by the blacksmith in the way he trims the hoof and by the balance and weight of the shoe.

The show horse is taught to change gaits only upon command or signal from the rider. He is expected to lead with the inside shoulder on every turn and change leads instantly if necessary or when asked. Signal for

"walk-trot," is noted for its extreme collection and action, while the five-gaited has extreme speed and action. "Collection" means that complete aliveness which comes from the impulse of the horse to go as opposed to the restraint of the rider to hold him back. The horse is on the bit, neck arched, legs well under him, and moving in fiery elegance. The height of collection would be a horse in a high-stepping canter, yet never

the trot is to lay a hand on the crest halfway up. To canter on a left lead the rider leans forward over the left side of the withers and pulls the horse's head slightly to the right, or more simply, a touch of the toe on the horse's left shoulder if he's been so taught.

Great show stables are the backbone of the Saddle Horse industry. They maintain a staff from manager and trainer on down to stable boys and pay extremely high prices for top horses. But why not, when you stop to realize that it takes several years to train an outstanding show horse—if you can find one to begin with. A Saddler that can win at big shows like the American Royal, Chicago International, the Kentucky State Fair or at Madison Square Garden command prices well into five figures—$25,000 not being exceptional and $50,000 and higher for a great champion stallion.

To come up with an outstanding show horse a breeder has to produce many that fall short of the top. These are sold off as minor-show competitors and for pleasure mounts. Once a great prospect is found, the training is long and involved and more exacting than that of any other breed of horse. He must develop one gait at a time, first the walk, then the trot, slow gait, rack, finally the canter and gallop which are the same except for speed. He must learn true gaits and do them with speed. Nor can he be conditioned to the lean point of race horses because he must keep enough flesh to be in "full bloom" and attractive to the eye.

To condition a trained Saddle Horse for a show all casual or pleasure riding is suspended. The horse is worked daily in a ring or on a runway for a minimum of thirty days before the event. During this time he is not allowed to take a single step that is not collected and animated, nor can he change gaits without a signal or command from the rider. At first he must perform his gaits in perfect form, later the speed can be built up. Again, shoeing is of great importance. Done properly, it can prevent or overcome minor defects and also give action. Faithful daily care brings out the coat sheen. The flowing mane and tail are never combed and seldom brushed, but usually worked by hand and finger.

The tail of every three- and five-gaited show horse is artificially set so it will be highly arched. Simply explained, there are four muscles which move the tail: the upper one raises it, the lower one pulls it down, the right and left move it in those directions. Thus when a veterinarian cuts the lower muscle of the tail, it cannot be pulled down and the constant tension of the upper muscle keeps the tail at a high level. After this is done, the tail is placed in a "set" (a kind of bent pipe with a harness) during the nonworking hours and held at proper show position.

Just prior to entering the show ring all three- and five-gaited and fine-harness horses have a wad of ginger inserted into the anus to bring the tail to its highest pitch while showing.

77

Wing Commander—five-gaited world champion

Many condemn Saddle Horse people for resorting to these props, and even call them brutal, but they generally speak without appreciation of the purpose. As we said earlier, the Saddle Horse is like the ballet dancer. His performance is an act designed to create beauty, and whatever can be used to bring out the aesthetic qualities are, in the minds of most, justified. In fact, every event, horse or otherwise, has its props. These are accoutrements necessary to the purpose of the event which, in the case of the Saddle Horse, is to produce the highest effect of beauty. This he does to a degree that no other horse can match.

As for the do-gooders who consider the Saddle Horse's props brutal, they would do a lot more good expending their energy toward some of the malpractices indulged in by racing men, especially at the lower levels of the so-called sport where lame horses are stood in ice water, shot with novocain, whipped and shocked electrically to charge them up for a cheap race. "What else can I do?" says the owner who claimed a horse for $10,000 only to find that he got a gimpy, unsound plug. "I can't sell him for dog food at seven cents a pound. I've got to protect my investment."

But to return to our subject of horse shows, the World's Grand Championship for the Saddle Horse is held at the Kentucky State Fair. It has never been won in less than forty-five minutes, usually extends to well over an hour, and has gone as long as two hours, during

Saddle Horse Dress—*Left:* Girl's amateur saddle suit with Kentucky jodhpurs   *Center:* Lady's formal tuxedo saddle suit   *Right:* Professional's saddle suit

which time the horses perform at all gaits, from the racing speed of the rack to the restrained majesty of the slow-gait.

The horses are also judged on conformation. Riders dismount, saddles are removed and horses judged on fineness, quality and presence, which means those bold show-horse ways and manners so distinct in the Saddle Horse.

Fine harness classes are also held for the Saddle Horse. In these he is shown to a four-wheel buggy with light harness and a snaffle bit, performs at an animated Park (slow) trot. He must move at a bold decisive step that is airy and classic. Most harness horses are trained exclusively for this phase of showing, but often a five-gaited horse competes in both divisions. Three-gaited Saddle Horses, because their manes and tails are clipped, cannot compete in harness events other than three-gaited combination ride-and-drive classes.

Today the major shows have developed a polish and professionalism not dreamed of by nineteenth-century Saddle Horse owners. Amateurs don't have a chance in the $10,000 stakes at Louisville, but they compete strongly in their own classes at big shows and especially at smaller ones throughout the country. At present there are more than five hundred shows recognized by the American Horse Shows Association, an increase of over 100 percent during the past two decades.

Riding in a Gaited Class is an exciting experience.

Saddle Horse tack

Double bridle with snaffle and curb bits

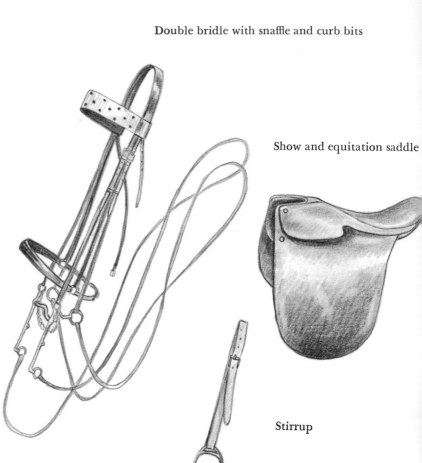

Show and equitation saddle

Stirrup

You must be absolutely familiar with your mount from months of previous training and riding. For the class itself you dress to the teeth and have your horse groomed to perfection. Then you go on stage and give it all you've got in manners, precision and style. The Saddle Horse wins for a kind of performance he and his rider could not do on a trail ride. Today's great show horse is a dramatic performer, not a beast of burden. After a show horse has won his triumphs on the tanbark he can retire and become the perfect pleasure mount.

Some of the great Saddle Horse stallions of the past are Black Squirrel, Cromwell, Harrison Chief, Rex McDonald, Bourbon Chief and Rex Peavine. Outstanding mares in their time were Gypsy Queen, Edna May and Hazel Dawn. Roxie Highland, a three-gaited mare, won 257 firsts out of 260 times shown and earned a total of $65,000 in eight years of showing back in the late 1920's.

Old Rex McDonald, foaled in 1890, is considered by many to be the greatest stallion of all. In recent times Wing Commander has been outstanding, winning six World Grand Championships in a row, 1948-53, while five to ten years of age.

Today between 2,000 and 2,500 Saddle Horses are registered annually by the American Saddle Horse Breeders Association in Louisville, Kentucky. They come from every state in the union and from several foreign countries, particularly South Africa. During the last thirty years exportations have been made consistently to that country and the breed has become very popular as a show horse and practical riding and driving horse on large farms and ranches.

The Saddle Horse is not merely the showpiece that most people consider him, but a glorious riding horse under all normal conditions. When his feet are cut down and he is shod lightly he makes an outstanding pleasure horse, sure-footed, with superbly comfortable gaits and classic beauty. On the bridle path he has natural action that is round and free, not excessively high like the coach horse nor the low-swinging stride of the Thoroughbred. His trot and canter are springy and exhilarating, not merely nondescript shuffles. He is alert to hazards, and because of superb balance he can shift his weight easily to meet whatever situation arises.

The show-ring Saddle Horse is no mount for a beginner. In fact he is dangerous, for the green rider may accidentally do something that will send the horse off at a gait or speed completely unanticipated, possibly causing a calamity. But as a pleasure mount he is gentle and strong, with almost intuitive responses.

Many Saddle Horses have become fine hunters and jumpers, and some Western ranches have successfully used them for stock horses, for they have great stamina and intelligence. On the hunting Saddler, no special forward seat is necessary to save delicate loins. They have strong backs and stout legs to carry weight.

But it will always be in the tanbark-covered show ring that the American Saddle Horse will be at his zenith, performing with animation and beauty never before equaled in the history of the horse world. No more glorious sight exists in horsedom of power, speed and movement than the Saddle Horse, a masterpiece of the art of horse breeding in America.

9.

The Tennessee Walking Horse

ALTHOUGH ALL BREEDS OF LIGHT HORSES HAVE GROWN IN the last twenty years, two in particular have really snowballed. One is the Quarter Horse, representing the world of Western riding and which we have already discussed, the other is the Tennessee Walking Horse, coming from the world of saddle breeds and show riding.

For the last five years the Tennessee Walker has ranked fourth among the highest annual registries, below the Thoroughbred, Standardbred and Quarter Horse, but he has been first among all the saddle breeds, considerably above his nearest rival, the Saddle Horse.

How can a horse that was only recognized as a breed

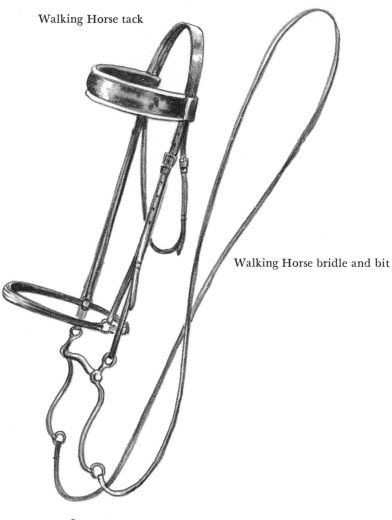

Walking Horse tack

Walking Horse bridle and bit

by the U.S. Department of Agriculture in February 1950 already have become the most popular saddle horse in the country? There are three good reasons:

He has the smoothest, least tiring gaits of any horse in the world.

His disposition is extremely kind, and this, combined with his easy gaits, makes him a comfortable, safe horse for people of all ages, young and old, both for pleasure and for show riding.

And because he's gentle by nature he's an ideal horse to keep in a backyard stable. He won't kick the walls down and try to buck Junior or Mother off even though he has not been exercised for a few days.

Don't get the idea that he's a soggy, listless horse. Not at all. He has a smooth, gliding way of moving that is full of animation. The big differences are his tractable disposition and easy gaits that make him tireless to ride. He has no bouncy trot that beginners find so hard to master and that even wearies professionals after a time. His gaits are three: a walk, running walk and canter.

The walk is a slick four-beat step done squarely and flat-footed but with more than average speed. The ordinary horse walks three to five miles an hour. A show Tennessee Walker will breeze along at six to nine miles an hour, a pleasure Walker slightly less.

The running walk is this horse's famous gait and it is so smooth that you can carry a glass of water in your hand and not spill a drop. The sensation is that of

World Ch. Midnight Sun

gliding along at high speed in a canoe over a calm lake. The gait is still square and four-cornered, but the rear foot now overreaches the track of the front foot on the same side from twelve to thirty inches. The faster the speed as in a show horse, the greater the overreach. The running walk can be done by show Walkers at twelve to sixteen miles an hour while pleasure Walkers hit eight to twelve miles an hour. The reason for the distinction between pleasure and show Walkers is that in the last few years show-ring professionals have pushed the Walker's speed beyond that of the pleasure animal. Over a long-distance haul like a fifty- or hundred-mile trail ride the pleasure speed would be more accurate.

As the Tennessee Walker sails along in his running walk he nods his head up and down (he is often called a nodder), a motion that acts as a counterweight and takes most of the movement out of the back, resulting in smoothness.

Among gaited-horse people the running walk is a very hot issue. Some claim that it is only a modified pace; others that it is an out-and-out rack. Actually it is between the two. When you ride a pacing horse there is great side movement. You feel as though you're doing the twist or the hula. In the rack there is the same four-beat rhythm of the running walk, but the horse works its head from side to side as if saying no while the Walker nods up and down saying yes. When the Saddle Horse racks, he seems to fly over the ground, whereas

85

the Tennessee Walker, in his running walk, appears to hug the ground.

The canter of a well-trained Walker is again something to behold, and better yet to ride. It is a slow, uniform roll which gives the rider a comfortable rise-and-fall ride and is called a "rocking-chair" gait. The rear legs are not lifted high, but the front quarters have extreme action, the head rolls rhythmically and the chin is well tucked. Again there is comfortable gait and a canter as beautiful as any you'll ever see.

One of the great attributes of the Tennessee Walker, beyond his riding comfort, is his most-amiable disposition. He is extremely gentle and even-tempered, which makes him an ideal mount for women and children, beginners and elderly people and also for those middle-aged businessmen who like to ride but who don't like to climb on a high-spirited steed and have to fight him the first half hour before he becomes a pleasure horse. At the same time he can be shown with all the class and pomp of a Saddle Horse while being, at this stage, a lot cheaper.

Many horse lovers of other breeds chide the Tennessee Walker as being an old-man's horse. It isn't at all. It is only a pleasure-horse supreme.

As for his having a kindly instead of a fiery disposition, this has worked to his advantage just as it has with the Quarter Horse. America's two fastest-growing breeds share the same disposition. They are comfort-able riding horses of high intelligence with a classy way of doing their job. Because they are basically safe they can be enjoyed by all ages, especially those who are not outstanding athletes.

And because the Tennessee Walker is calm and collected he makes an ideal home-stable horse. A twelve-year-old can walk into the stall, lead him out, curry and clean him, put on the saddle and go for a ride all in relative safety. In many cases whole families have taken up Walking Horses, riding together, going to shows together to compete in the variety of classes from Twelve-and-Under to Fifty-and-Over as well as Parent-and-Child.

What's the background of this remarkable horse? Is he a Johnny-come-lately? Far from it. He dates back more than 175 years to the same origins as the Saddle Horse. Again, it was a matter of selection for a specialized use, namely to get around the countryside on horseback with as much ease and reasonable speed as possible.

The breed originated in the Middle Basin of Tennessee, where native blue grass grows thick in the limestone and phosphate soil. The story begins with pioneers moving westward from Virginia and the Carolinas on easy-gaited stock descended from old Narragansett and Canadian pacer blood. As the frontier solidified itself in the lush rolling hills of Tennessee, Thoroughbreds from Virginia and Kentucky were crossed into the walking stock. The people did so much riding that they

ad ever seen in one contest. In those days the Walk-
Horse, after competing in his own class, would enter
Saddle Horse divisions and often win there. He
and still is a multigaited horse, as will be explained
r.

great addition to the Walking Horse breed came
ugh Allan F-1, a registered Standardbred who was
ed in 1886 and died in 1910. This handsome black
ion, now recognized as Foundation Sire Number
by the Tennessee Walking Horse Registry, carried
finest trotting blood of his day. On his sire's side he
a close descendant of George Wilkes, Hambleto-
and Mambrino Chief, while his dam was of the
Black Hawk Morgan blood. At a time when every-
wanted trotters, Allan could only pace, hence he
a failure at harness racing.

1891 he was sold from his home in Lexington,
ucky, for $355 to a man in Murfreesboro, Tennes-
After that, as it so often has happened with great
, he had many owners, always at a cheaper price,
re someone recognized his worth. Once he was
d for a yearling filly, a Jersey heifer and twenty
rs. At the ebb of his career he was used to tease
on a mule-breeding farm. Finally in 1903, when
as seventeen years old, James R. Brantley bought
for $110, recognizing in him the potential of a
Walking Horse sire. His bloodline was outstand-
his conformation without a fault and his gaits,

which included the running walk, effortless and graceful.

Soon he was being bred to the best mares in Bedford,
Coffee, Cannon, Rutherford and Franklin counties,
heartland of the Tennessee Walking Horse. Among his
celebrated offspring were Hunter's Allen F-10, Red
Allen F-33, King Allen F-34, the famous mare Merry
Legs F-4 and the most celebrated of all, Roan Allen
F-38. (The letter F signifies foundation stock of the
Tennessee Walking Horse, there being 114 sires and
dams so listed by the registry when it was organized in
1935. For some unknown reason the heirs of Allan F-1
all spell their names Allen.)

Roan Allen F-38 was a superhorse, spectacular as a
performer and without a peer as a producer. He was
one of the few seven-gaited horses the world has ever
known, capable of doing the flat walk, running walk,
canter, a perfect square-trot, fox-trot, pace and rack.
Often Roan Allen competed in walking, fine-harness
and gaited classes all in one show. Many times he won
in five-gaited competition, but first and foremost he was
a Walking Horse and a sire of Walking Horses. His
heirs have dominated the show world ever since he died
in 1930.

The dynasty of Allan F-1 is responsible for bringing
the quality of consistency to the Tennessee Walking
Horse. Before its arrival, Walkers came in all shapes,
sizes and colors. The gaits were well fixed but there was

wanted a comfortably gaited horse. The one they developed walked as fast as the average trot, even canter, and hours of continuous riding left neither horse nor rider tired.

In the early 1800's Andrew Jackson wrote of a horse named Free and Easy, whose gaits were like his name, being sent to North Carolina for breeding purposes. He also mentioned the great Canadian stallion *Copperbottom, coming back from North Carolina at the age of twenty to live out his life in Tennessee. Old *Copperbottom figures prominently in Saddle Horse bloodlines and added significantly to the Tennessee Walker as did Traveler, Tom Hal, Grey John, Mountain Slasher, Snow Heels, Pat Malone, Cockspur, Denmark and others. Traveler is said to have sired forty-seven horses in General Forrest's Cavalry and not one of them was lost during the Civil War.

During the Reconstruction days the Tennessee Walker carried the circuit rider to rural churches to preach, the country doctor on his round of visits, children to and from one-room schools and beaux to court their belles. And many a log-cabin mother rode the family Walker swiftly into town carrying a basket of eggs on her arm to exchange for salt, sugar and coffee.

By 1875 infusions of Thoroughbred, Arabian and Saddle blood had taken place, and the comfortable, swift "running walk" had become a fixed characteristic of the breed. At this time they were called Plantation

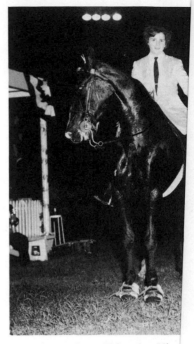

Fair Warning ridden by Virg[inia], juvenile world champion, 196[2]

Horses and had spread to [...] throughout the South. Bu[t...] their home. Here they wer[e...] in 1887 a Walking Horse [...] Fair had fifty-seven entrie[s...] later, said that it was the fi[...]

Judging Tennessee Walking Class

wide variation in looks, ways of going and speed. To-day, thanks to the descendants of Allan F-1 and con-centrated breeding efforts, the Walking Horse has be-come a consistent type. He weighs from 1,000 to 1,200 pounds and stands around 15½ hands. Black is the great show color, but they come in sorrel, chestnut, all kinds of roans, white, bay, brown, gray, palomino and even spotted, although these last are nearly always un-registered stock. White markings on head and legs are common.

The Tennessee Walker is a solidly built horse. His shoulders and breast and hind quarters are well muscled. He has a short back and a barrel chest, his neck is thick and muscled from the nodding action of the running walk. Although Saddle Horse blood shows in his high head, lively facial expression and proud grace, he has none of the delicate refinement of that breed, but is a horse of real substance from dense leg bones to the power of his whole body. His head has an intelligent look contained in the wide skull and eyes, the upper lid of which is often wrinkled. His move-ments glisten with style, rhythm and beauty, and it is for all of these qualities that audiences have become in-creasingly fond of this distinguished horse when he

The Walking Horse gait

takes to the show ring. His forelock and first-mane lock are braided with ribbons in the colors of his stable. He generally carries an artificially set tail, and his long mane flies like a flag when he turns on his running walk.

Top show for the Walking Horse is the National Celebration held each year in the little town of Shelbyville, Tennessee. To this unofficial capital of the Walking Horse world each September come trucks, trailers and planes bringing horses, contestants and viewers for the six-day event which culminates in a World's Grand Champion. Total attendance amounts to more than sixty thousand people, and although professionals vie for the big stakes, it is the amateurs who make up more than half the show. This trend is a healthy sign, for the

Walking Horse is so easy to ride that the amateur, old or young, can compete to the hilt. Judging in the big-stakes classes is done on the following recommended scale: 20 percent for the flat walk, 20 percent for the canter, 40 percent for the running walk and 20 percent for conformation. With some judges the running walk receives a higher consideration. Equitation for the amateur is receiving more and more attention.

Proof of the Walking Horse's smooth, tireless-to-the-rider gaits is the fact that all bird-dog trainers use them. The men whose business it is to train pointers and setters spend a great part of their lives working these dogs from horseback. They wouldn't be caught dead on anything but a Walking Horse. Each trainer has at least two, sometimes half a dozen, depending upon the size of his operation, and he'll haul them hundreds of miles to a field trial just to have good mounts. These horses ground tie the moment you slide out of the saddle. They're not afraid of gun shots, don't step on the dogs and learn a score of little tricks which valuably assist the trainer. Above all, they work—long hours every day.

Because the Walker is a mélange of many other breeds and can perform several gaits when urged to, he is generally trained until he understands clearly what is wanted. It's not unusual to see a foal instinctively swing into a running walk to keep up with his mother as she moves across a pasture, so the teaching is not an arduous process as with the Saddle Horse. Some youngsters have trotty instincts and are the easiest to teach. Those which are inclined to pace require more patience and time but in the end the quality of their gaits is noticeably superior. By learning the true running walk and rocking-chair canter the horse automatically develops the smoothness for which he is famous. Another good thing is that once his gaits have been established, which means bringing them to the fore above all the others he has inherited, he does not forget them. Naturally the show horse trains harder and longer, for he must develop greater speed and action than the pleasure horse.

The Tennessee Walkers' popularity has been concentrated in the South and Midwest, those areas which have known and used him the longest. It has now spread to Texas, California and the Northwest and is just beginning to reach the East. Dude-ranchers have started to use Walkers, for they realize the majority of guests are not great riders and don't care to be jounced around on a billy-goat horse. He's fine for trail rides because he's sure-footed, and as time goes on will undoubtedly make a strong showing in endurance rides, for he has the bottom and the gaits.

No doubt the Tennessee Walker will continue to flourish, for he's earned his title of Mr. Pleasure Horse not through advertising promotion but from what he has to offer. All things being considered, he's most likely to stick.

10.

The Appaloosa

About twenty-five years ago there arose in the Pacific Northwest a very pleasant malady called "spotted fever." It began when the Appaloosa Horse Club was organized in Moscow, Idaho, for the purpose of reviving a strain of Indian horse that was all but extinct. With little more than enthusiasm to go on, the club began publicizing the history of this uniquely colored horse, started a registry to maintain bloodlines and issue pedigrees, encouraged breeding, began a monthly magazine, sponsored the first National Appaloosa Horse Show in 1948, the first registered Appaloosa auction in 1949, and managed to register 262 horses in 1954 and a

Roping with Appaloosa

whopping 7,343 in 1961. Today there are more than 25,000 registered from almost every state in the Union.

"Spotted fever" is the term used by enthusiastic followers of the Appaloosa, for the horse's distinctive markings consist of spots, usually on a white blanket across the rump, and the feverish pace at which the Appaloosa's popularity has been growing is little short of epidemic. The annual National Appaloosa Show is a five-hundred-horse, five-day event which includes all categories of halter classes, reining, Western pleasure,

pairs, roping and hunter classes, stakes races of ⅛, ¼, ⅜ and ½ mile, an elaborate costume division, stump racing, stakes racing, rope racing and a Nez Percé Buffalo Hunting event using live buffaloes. Youngsters, adults and professionals all compete for a heap of prizes.

Membership in the Appaloosa Horse Club has grown to more than five thousand, representing almost the entire United States as well as Canada and Mexico. Appaloosa breeding ranches and farms have sprung up in every state west of the Mississippi, several in the

South and East. There are now nearly fifty registered Appaloosa auctions annually. Just about every worthwhile horse show in the country contains at least one Appaloosa class, and several regional shows are held exclusively for the breed with championships in halter and performance divisions. Sixty-three percent are used for stock, racing and rodeos, 30 percent for pleasure riding and the balance for parade, jumping, drill and high school work. Prices for a high-quality Appaloosa start around $2,000 and go up to $15,000 or better—all this for the only breed of horse ever developed by the American Indian. The Nez Percé nation of the Northwest is credited with being the only primitive people on the North American continent practicing animal husbandry to the extent of fixing a distinct type of horse— the beautiful, strong and highly respected Appaloosa, which they loved so dearly that they lost their nation fighting to save it.

The average horseman tends to consider the Appaloosa only a color. Actually it is a separate breed easily recognized by its markings. Appaloosa blood shows itself in six different types of markings and five different physical characteristics. The color types range from a dark-bodied horse with a white rump or a blanket which is spotted, to the light gray or white horse covered with spots and called a leopard or polka-dot. No particular size, number or pattern of spots is required, but they must be spots and not patches like the Pinto

Dressage horse

Photo: Appaloosa Horse Club

has. The physical characteristics which almost always show themselves in the Appaloosa are thin mane, thin brush tail, eye encircled by white like the human eye, skin mottled around the nostrils and reproductive organs, and the hoofs striped vertically black and white. The horse comes in all basic colors, the most dramatic being black or sorrel with the spotted white blanket.

To understand the exceptional rise in spotted fever we must look at the history of this most unusual and remarkable horse.

First of all, he is one of the oldest breeds recorded by

94

man. Horses of the polka-dot, or leopard-spotted, variety appear in Persian art of the fourteenth century and in Chinese art dating back to 500 B.C. Thus it would appear that the horse originally came out of China or Mongolia either as a trader's mount or on the tides of war. Always an eye-catcher because of its markings, the spotted animal was probably in high demand wherever it went. Eventually and inevitably it reached Spain, where stock-raising culture was one of the highest in the world during the fourteenth, fifteenth and sixteenth centuries. When Spaniards brought horses to the New World and established elaborate breeding farms in Hispaniola, Cuba and Jamaica, the spotted horse was included and later became part of the mustang herd that covered the West and supplied the Indians with mounts for the first time in their history, about 1700.

Still the spotted horse had not received its present-day name. That came about through the Nez Percé Indians who inhabited the fertile Palouse land bordering the Snake River, where the states of Washington, Idaho and Oregon all come together. The Nez Percé Indians were a settled tribe subsisting on fishing and agriculture until they obtained the horse about 1730. They took a fancy to those of the spotted variety, bred them skillfully for speed, color and conformation—blue roan with a white blanket was their favorite—disposed of the inferior offspring by gelding or barter and, within a hundred years, had a distinct type of animal

The Appaloosa was an old Indian horse. This is an 1875 photo.

that was strong and intelligent, friendly and beautiful, and highly respected by early Western horsemen.

The Nez Percé Indian, like the Arab, was a great horseman, treated his mount with pride and care, rearing a colt or filly as part of his family, and he would never part with the best of his horses at any price short of death. With his spotted horse he took to roaming far beyond the Snake River, into Montana's buffalo

95

Scene at Meridian Appaloosa Horse Show

country. The spotted horse traveled at full gallop among the rugged mountains and valleys, his master glued to his back. The Indian had no saddle and, to hunt buffalo, needed both hands free for his bow and arrow, so he taught his horse to cut in close for the shot, then to pull away from the wounded lunging beast. Thus the Appaloosa, like all Indian mustangs, learned the simple rudiments which later were to be applied to cattle. The most intelligent were bred to one another so that quality and ability were always improved.

When Lewis and Clark came upon the Nez Percé tribe in 1805, their population was estimated at about six thousand people and their horses were described as being of rare beauty and outstanding quality. The Palouse River drained the rich land which nurtured the Nez Percé and his horse. The area became known as Palouse Country and the mounts of the Nez Percé were called Palouse horses. The word was slurred into "Apalouse," then "Apalousie" and finally "Appaloosa," as it stands today. But this is only a small part of the story. The tragedy still remains.

As settlers moved into the Northwest it was inevitable that they take over the rich grazing pastures between the Palouse and Clearwater rivers, both of which drain into the famous Snake River. As the plow cut up the land, Indians were herded onto reservations to get them out of the way. Then in 1860 someone found a nugget of gold. Wagon trains flooded across the Bonanza Trail bringing greedy gold seekers. Treaties were broken by the law of the rifle, though the Nez Percé Indian wanted nothing more than to live in peace and raise spotted horses and cattle on the land that had been his.

In 1875 General O. O. Howard, U.S. commandant of the region, ordered all Nez Percé Indians onto a reservation so shrunken that there was insufficient room for their cattle and thousands of spotted horses. The Indians resisted, knowing it might mean extinction. In 1876 the Wallowa band of Nez Percé rounded up its stock and crossed the churning Snake River as it boiled through Hell's Canyon at the height of the June flood. Hundreds of cows, calves and colts were drowned and hundreds more stolen by pursuing whites.

General Howard ordered his troops to bring the renegade band into line and sent 110 soldiers against a camp guarded by 65 warriors, but the Nez Percé Indians defeated the troops through superior horsemanship. Howard, fearing that a successful Indian revolt would arouse other restless and unruly tribes throughout the West, vowed to wipe out the band. Some 500 soldiers, packers and scouts pursued the Nez Percé and fought battles at Cottonwood and Clearwater with no decisive outcome. The Indians then took to the mountains and followed the Lolo trail across the backbone of Idaho into Montana, where they believed safety lay

waiting. They thought their war was against General Howard, not the whole United States, and if they escaped his department they would be free.

The Lolo trail was a nightmare of jagged mountains and near-impassable forests without pasture. The march, led by Chief Joseph, began with 190 men, more than 400 women and children, cattle, and a horse herd estimated at 3,000 head. They averaged an incredible sixteen miles a day, but horses became lost, and many starved for want of pasture land and dropped off into ravines to die of broken legs.

Finally plunging out of the wilderness into Montana, the Nez Percé band saw a giant sweep of prairie, an ideal pasture for their prized horses and cattle. They made camp in a pine grove near Big Hole River to rest and nurse their wounds. The men would hunt, the women would cut new lodge poles, and their cherished spotted horses would graze and grow sleek again.

An old man owned several horses and two young warriors asked him for fresh remounts to ride back over the trail to see if they had been followed. He refused. Thus no one saw the soldiers advancing on the encampment. At dawn the next morning occurred the famous Battle of Big Hole. The result was decimation for both sides, women and children slaughtered.

The Nez Percé band retreated back into the mountains, which seemed to be both their safety and their doom. Spotted horses carried the wounded, the aged, the women, children and weary warriors. The band made raids for supplies, killed crippled horses and ate them to keep from starving. They moved northward, fighting skirmish after skirmish, constantly losing horses and cattle and people. Canada became their goal, the land where Sitting Bull had found his peace. They were so sure of escape, sought it so desperately, but within fifty miles of the border the final blow was struck. They were surrounded and defeated, forced into surrender.

Hope and dignity were gone, but bitterest of all was the loss of their beloved spotted horses which had carried them faithfully for 1,300 desperate miles into oblivion. What remained of the huge herd was confiscated, driven to Fort Keogh on the Yellowstone and sold.

By 1880 the Nez Percé Appaloosa was scattered to the four winds. No one particularly cared about the horse's merit or attractiveness, so it took its place beside other stock horses doing ranch work throughout the West. Some cowpokes liked its flashy markings and rode the animal in parades, others made them into cutting and roping horses, and many ranch owners kept one or two for their kids to play with. As late as 1910 several men reported seeing excellent Appaloosas on various Northwest Indian reservations, the surviving remnants of the Nez Percé herd. And in the 1930's the Pine Ridge Indian Reservation in South Dakota bought a stallion in Oregon to improve and continue its strain of Appa-

loosas, some of which were originally shipped there from Fort Keogh after the bitter struggle.

Still, the Appaloosa managed to survive, mostly through the intricacies of genetics, for an Aappaloosa mare or stallion outcrossed to a Quarter Horse or Thoroughbred or just plain pinto cow pony often produced Appaloosa-type offspring—the polka-dot blanket over the hind quarters, the stubby brush tail and thin mane. Even a solid-colored mare bred to a solid-colored stallion might produce an Appaloosa if both carried enough of the genes. Appaloosa mares often pass as straight mares because they do not generally have the vivid colorations of the stallions.

Also, the breed always remained popular in the Northwest. Elders recalled the animal when it carried the Nez Percé proudly and swiftly. It had that something extra and thus was maintained in Washington, Oregon and Idaho by men who knew good horses.

The Appaloosa is one of the great versatile mounts we have today and this accounts to a considerable degree for its popularity. The horse has endurance, speed, intelligence, soundness and a color that is a trademark all its own. The animal can be trained effectively in all phases of Western rodeo work, it runs in flat races at Quarter Horse distances, jumps in hunter classes, looks beautiful in a parade or costume class and ordinarily has a fine, gentle disposition that makes it supersafe around children.

Appaloosa racing

Photo: Appaloosa Horse Club

South America also has quite a number of Appaloosas. Venezuela recently imported some of our best studs to cross into its blood, which was undoubtedly inherited from the original Spanish horse in the same manner that our mustang developed, the escaped stock bending southward instead of north. Brazil and Argentina also have the Appaloosa, introduced to those areas by early Spanish expeditions, and today private breeders in the United States often import brood mares from south of the border to strengthen our own blood. The South American Appaloosa tends to be of the leopard-spotted variety in markings and is particularly effective in throwing Appaloosas even when outcrossed to solid-colored stock.

The Appaloosa is still in evidence in parts of Europe, especially as a circus horse and performer in Austria, Hungary, Switzerland and the Netherlands. They are almost impossible to find in Spain.

Because of their dramatic markings, Appaloosas have appeared as noblemen's horses at various times in history. France's Louis XIV had a white leopard, and the Duke of Wellington's famous charger Copenhagen was painted by Ward with a spattering of snowflakes over his withers. The reason spotted horses haven't overrun the world is that when two are mated together their offspring will not necessarily be spotted. The valuable Appaloosa stallions of today possess the genetic strength to reproduce their color.

What has made the Appaloosa so popular? Partly the horse's versatility, partly his startling color and partly the Indian lore which has inevitably grown up around the horse. Several of the show classes embrace the traditions of the old Nez Percé tribe. Stakes racing is one example. Also the buffalo-hunting event in which the rider carries a long pole representing a hunting spear. The end is blunted by a paint-daubed rag, and he thrusts his spear into the buffalo's side just back of the foreleg in simulating a kill. The event is judged on time and accuracy.

For costume and parade classes youthful riders go to great lengths in researching details of Nez Percé costumes and habits. Magnificent war bonnets are made or bought, also blankets, leather skirts and blouses similar to those the squaws wore, and lances, breastplates and feather trimmings for the horse. Thus the Appaloosa has gained access to many of the great parades throughout the country, such as the gigantic Parada del Sol in Scottsdale, Arizona, which each year contains approximately four thousand horses of all breeds and stretches for three miles. The best male rider in 1962 was Bear-Step of Mt. Shadows, an Indian mounted on an Appaloosa called Apache Tears.

Many prizes at the annual National Appaloosa Horse Show are authentic Nez Percé lore, such as the beautiful Katouche, awarded to the champion two-year-old stallion.

Most Appaloosas range in weight from 950 to 1175 pounds and can be of any height above 14 hands at maturity, which is five years or over. The conformation standard is necessarily loose because the Appaloosa has

been crossed with many breeds and hence appears in several different types. Variations include the stock-horse type coming from a Quarter Horse cross, the racing and hunting type coming from a Thoroughbred cross, the parade type, the Arabian type, etc. In Appaloosa halter classes horses are judged 40 percent on conformation, 20 percent on type, 20 percent on soundness and 20 percent on action. Color docs not enter into it unless there are ties. The judge may then decide according to the best-marked animal. Western performance classes are operated under regular stock-horse rules.

The Appaloosa Horse Club has been a prime mover in bringing back the spotted horse. It has encouraged formation of regional clubs which have been instrumental in gaining Appaloosa classes at the major live-stock expositions, fairs and horse shows. They in turn sponsor regional shows, sales, trail rides and social functions through which Appaloosa owners are able to enjoy their horses fully.

Appaloosa horse racing is also becoming popular. The parent club has drawn up a set of rules and, at regional shows as well as certain Western tracks, Appaloosa racc horses make fine showings. Certain ones like the gelding J.O., who holds a track record at Platte City, Missouri, have been successful against the Quarter Horse and Thoroughbred to the extent that ranches are breeding the Appaloosa exclusively for racing.

Each year special cash prizes are offered for the outstanding Appaloosa cutting horse, and the parent club has a $5,000 prize for the first Appaloosa to climb within the National Cutting Horse Association's Top Ten of the Year. Special judging schools, reining, roping and cutting clinics are held at shows and fairs, and at almost every large meeting a professor lectures on genetics and the art of breeding for color.

Children especially love the Appaloosa for its kindly manners and unusual coloration. So do the breeders who have reaped a windfall in bringing back and vastly improving this unique pleasure horse. As someone said long ago, horses with a future come from horses with a past, and in this realm the Appaloosa certainly qualifies. This real fun horse will be with us in ever-increasing numbers from now on as the spotted fever spreads.

11.

The Palomino

When you glimpse your first palomino with its golden body and flowing white mane and tail, you will probably blink your eyes, have another look, then exclaim, "There's the most beautiful horse I've ever seen!" Certainly he is one of the most spectacular. And seldom does a parade go by that he does not head or appear many times in the line of march as a high-stepping showpiece.

Throughout history Palominos have been treated with an awe bordering on reverence. In Greek mythology nine golden stallions with nostrils flaring fire hauled Helios in his sun chariot daily over the world from east to west. The Pharaohs of ancient Egypt prized golden horses as did the Vikings and royalty of the Middle Ages. Whether these were similar to the Palomino of today we do not know but the golden horse, because of its exquisite beauty, has commanded a high price in any age. In fact, only nobility could afford them.

Where they came from originally has never been established. Some claim the Palomino was once a breed that disappeared as a result of outcrossing. More likely it was only a color that appeared at infrequent intervals, perhaps the result of an albino cross on a sorrel. The Palomino seems to be a close relative of the albino, for when two Palominos are bred together it is not unusual for them to produce an albino with its white eyes, pink-white skin and white feet.

Some of the Barb horses may have been palomino in color, or perhaps an albino Barb of Moorish origin was crossed to a Spanish sorrel, for we know that the great horse breeders of Spain produced outstanding ones. Queen Isabella loved these golden horses and the *Remuda Real* (the royal stables) had many to please her. They were called Isabellas in her court and served the royal carriage.

It is said that Cortez brought Palominos with him in his conquest of Mexico, but these were most likely duns. The color did appear in the mustang's ranks later, along with a hundred other hues, and the mustang came directly from the early Spanish conquistador's horse.

Bourbon's Golden King, Saddle Horse-type Palomino

Many tales and superstititions have attached themselves to the Palomino. His name alone has been traced to bottles of wine, pigeon dung, soiled chemises and California soldiers. Most likely, Spanish generals rode Palominos. There was one named Juan Palamia who supposedly rode a gleaming golden stallion into California to colonize the area for the Spanish. Whether this is the origin of the name is not known.

In any event the Palomino remains a beautiful horse, as much in demand today as he ever was. His ideal color

is that of a newly minted gold coin with white mane and tail, but he varies from burnt orange all the way to cream. Manes and tails run from silver through ivory to snow white. American Horse Show rules prohibit dyeing or bleaching the tails and manes, and no more than 15 percent dark hair is permissible. Some Palominos are dappled, others are not. California favors the solid, dark orange-gold, while Texas leans toward the dappled, lighter golden color.

Because the Palomino is basically only a color he has no fixed standard of conformation. There are Palominos of the Quarter Horse type in the Southwest; of the Arabian type in California, Washington and Oregon; of the Saddle Horse type in the East and Midwest; of the Walking Horse type in Tennessee and the South. Even Morgan horses occasionally come out Palomino.

To accommodate this great variety of conformation the two groups which register Palominos, the Palomino Horse Breeders of America and Palomino Horse Association, issue pedigrees only after inspection proves the horse to be of true coloration. He cannot have white body markings of the Pinto type, nor can he have blue, moon, pink or glassy eyes. White face markings and white socks, or stockings, are permitted.

Since the Palomino color appears in just about all breeds except the pure Arabian and Thoroughbred, many horses today have dual registry. A registered Quarter Horse that is palomino in color may, after passing inspection, be registered also as a Palomino and compete in the halter and performance classes which are held at Palomino shows. In fact, more and more dual champions are beginning to appear. This means a horse has gained his championship within his breed, then enters the Palomino world and gains a title there.

All-Palomino horse shows are springing up through-

movement similar to the slow-gait, dramatic but uncomfortable to ride.

Tack for a parade horse is beautiful beyond belief and just as expensive. Saddles are silver mounted. Handworked silver *tapaderos* cover the stirrups and an ornate breast collar depicts scenes in silver. A magnificent *serape* of ornate silver design drapes over the horse's loins halfway to the ground. Even the bridle and reins are coated with silver. Parade saddles start at $1,000 and go up. Roy Rogers has a saddle which contains 1,400 ounces of silver, 136 ounces of gold, 1,500 rubies and is valued at $50,000.

Breeding the Palomino presents many problems. This golden animal is in high demand, but the trick is to produce a good horse with the desired color. As we said earlier, two Palominos do not necessarily produce a Palomino foal. If they did, the horse would easily be developed into a breed and a higher standard of type would result. Scientists are inclined to believe that Palominos contain a dilution factor in their genetic make-up which tends to dissolve their color when they are mated. Breeders agree that "golden horses" come chiefly from three matings: Palomino to sorrel (this produces the highest percentage—50 percent); Palomino to Palomino; and albino to chestnut or sorrel. However, in recent years the color has become more strongly fixed in certain stallions and mares, so breeders are naturally moving to this blood.

out the country. The larger ones usually divide the halter classes into stock-horse and pleasure types to simplify the judging. The performance division includes all kinds of Western riding and competition as well as gaited classes, pleasure classes and especially parade classes. Palominos make great parade horses. They show at two gaits: the flat-footed walk, which is animated, and the parade gait, a beautiful high-stepping

One thing is certain, the golden Palomino will always be popular. He is a showpiece de luxe whether turning in a drill team or performing at a horse show. And when they come marching down the street, people will "Oh!" and "Ah-h-h . . ." as they have since parades first began.

THE PINTO, OR PAINT, WHICH MOST OF US THINK OF AS
an old Indian horse, is really an ancient strain dating
back to Biblical times and before. Pinto horses graced
the walls of Egyptian tombs 3,000 years ago. They appeared in early Chinese art, in Persian tapestries and in
cave drawings of primitive man. Horses of splashed and
spotted markings are historically recorded in Spain in
the fifth century.

The Spanish favored bright-colored mounts and they
brought the Pinto along with so many other colored
horses to the New World as *conquistador* mounts.
The ancient records of Diaz del Castillo, historian for
Cortez, show that two Pintos were included in the
original sixteen horses Cortez took with him to Mexico

12.
The Pinto

in 1519. Though these horses all died or were lost, it verifies the fact that the strain existed then and undoubtedly was produced on the horse-breeding ranches of Jamaica and Hispaniola, later reached the mainland and escaped to become another facet of the mustang.

The Pinto's unusual coloration is believed to be the result of the combined action of albino, melano and erythemic genes (white, black and red) on the skin. The horses frequently have glass or blue eyes and other albino characteristics. Its color is a trait which geneticists say was probably present in the earliest beginnings of the horse. It is definitely not the result of crosses between solid-colored horses. If that were the case, just about all the horses in the world today would be Pintos.

The word comes from the Spanish *Pintado,* meaning painted. It refers to horses patterned in two colors—white and almost anything else from black to cream. Because the colors are distinctive and highly contrasting, the horses are always flashy eye-catchers. Over the years many terms sprang up to describe the various Pinto color combinations. "Piebald" meant black and white and was the favorite among Pinto enthusiasts. "Skewbald" was white with any other color but black. "Calico," "spotted" and "paint" were also used by old-time Westerners, but all these terms are being abandoned in favor of a more accurate color description.

Today the breed is divided into two types: the "Tobiano" and the "Overo." The Tobiano type of Pinto appears more frequently in North America and Europe, the Overo in Asia and South America. Sometimes it takes a good eye to tell the difference though no two Pintos are ever marked the same.

In theory the Tobiano is a dark-colored horse with white markings, while the Overo is a white horse with dark markings, but this distinction is not as obvious as it sounds. The simplest way to tell one from the other is by comparing the top line with the bottom line (the line of the back with the line of the belly).

On the Tobiano, the white filters down from the top line as if someone had poured a can of white paint on his back. The head is nearly always dark, with a star, stripe or blaze. The dark color often includes the neck and chest. The legs will probably be white from the knees or hocks down. The mane and tail will be the color from which they stem. As a rule the Tobiano's spots are larger and more sharply defined. Glassy eyes are infrequent.

In the Overo, the white tends to flow upwards from the bottom line, or underside, of the horse as if someone had turned him on his back and poured white paint on his belly. The belly will be white while the back, mane and tail will generally be dark. The Overo's markings are more jagged, to the point where the zigzags may resemble "lightning." The head is often white or bald. Glassy or blue eyes are common.

The distinction between Tobiano and Overo is in

The Davis family of San Diego, California, on their three parade Pintos

color only and has no bearing upon quality or ability. The Tobiano is generally a more pleasing horse to look at because the color patterns are smoother and less jagged than the Overo. The Pinto strain has considerable potency and reproduces itself consistently. Thus the splashed markings can be found or produced in horses of nearly every breed, although none of the other breeds will accept horses of Pinto color for registry.

Because the Pinto's historical roots in America came from the mustang, few horsemen considered him of high caliber. He was an Indian pony good for rodeos, circuses and parades, but that didn't cut much ice with ranchers who wanted a doer, not a looker. However, the Pinto has always been a tough, sturdy horse who did a good job wherever and whenever he was asked to.

Since none of the other breeds would accept Pintos for registration, the strain began to decline before the onslaught of pedigreed horses. Finally a group led by George Glendenning formed in September 1941 what is today known as the Pinto Horse Association of America with headquarters in Connecticut. Aims were to perpetuate, improve and develop this colorful horse. Breeders and trainers were encouraged to the point that the Pinto in recent years has taken on new quality and beauty never before attained. The demand for high-quality Pintos now outreaches the supply, and two other competing registries have been formed: the American Pinto Horse Association in California and the American Paint Stock Horse Association in Texas. In 1962 the Pinto was recognized as a breed by the U.S. Department of Agriculture.

The Pinto of today is a multipurpose light horse, and a good one too. The stock-horse type is easily trained for Western competition like roping and reining and cutting, also trail riding and pleasure classes. He has halter classes at his own shows, he jumps, is used in harness classes, parade classes, barrel racing and English pleasure riding. Even the President's wife, Mrs. Jacqueline Kennedy, hunts with a colorful Pinto upon occasion.

Says one Pinto registry about the horse, "Modern Pintos of the Americas have degrees of excellence which match the endurance and intelligence of the Arabian; the general utility of the Morgan; the work ability and 'cow sense' of the stock horse, as well as the docility and usefulness of the children's pony."

Don't ever doubt that a staunch heart lies beneath the Pinto's splashy coat. Several years ago a man named Tschiffeley rode two Argentine Criolos from Buenos Aires to Washington, D.C., approximately 10,000 miles through jungles, deserts, swamps, across plains and over mountains. One of these horses was a Pinto.

Another man named Frank Hopkins took his stallion from Laramie, Wyoming, to Paris to compete in the 1899 World's Fair. Afterward he was asked to enter the 3,000-mile endurance race held annually in Arabia for several centuries. Starting at Aden in Arabia and riding into Syria across deserts and mountains, then swinging back to Arabia, Hopkins and his cream and white Pinto finished in sixty-eight days and won by thirty-three hours, the only horse other than an Arabian ever to win this historic race.

The age-old Pinto still has what it takes, as the public is beginning to find out, and in years to come this horse will certainly make a bigger name for himself, a name based on quality, class and ability as well as lavish color.

13.

... and some
other breeds

SEVERAL LESSER BREEDS HAVE APPEARED ON THE HORIZON
in recent years, the result of imports from foreign
countries and the efforts of some people to produce new
types of horses.

One of these latter is the American albino, a pure
white horse with pink skin. This breed came about
chiefly through the efforts of C.R. and H.B. Thompson
who, in 1918, purchased a white stallion which they
crossed with a band of Morgan-Arabian mares. Over a
period of years they succeeded in establishing a strain
of true albino horse which reproduces with considerable regularity.

Most white horses are actually grays turned white

with age. They are recognizable by their dark skin, which is most obvious around the nostrils and lips and reproductive area. The albino is clearly pink-skinned in these places as well as under his hair.

He has been used extensively as a parade horse and for exhibition work such such as Roman riding and jumping. Many officials, dignitaries and dictators have ridden albinos in flashy displays before crowds. He's a highly intelligent animal that is reliable and consistent.

The Fox-Trot Horse comes from the Ozark country of Missouri and might well be called an off-shoot of the Tennessee Walker because his origin and purpose are about the same. His ancestors—Morgan, Arabian, Thoroughbred, Saddle Horse and Tennessee Walker—came from Virginia, Tennessee and Kentucky as easy-gaited settler stock.

His best-known gait, the fox-trot, is easy for both rider and horse and is a variation of the plantation walk. It is a broken gait. The horse walks with his front feet and trots with his hind feet. When done properly, the track of the back feet lands squarely on the track of the front feet.

The Missouri Fox-Trotter, as he is best known, nods his head with each step in the same manner as the Tennessee Walker. He is a compact, well-muscled horse with a wide range of colors from black, bay and sorrel through white. Chestnut sorrels with white markings are most favored. The horse shows without artificial tail sets, is sometimes five-gaited but in the show ring performs only the flat-footed walk, fox-trot and canter. Most of the horse shows in the Missouri-Oklahoma area have fox-trotting classes and the breed has a registry.

In 1732 Frederick Wilhelm I, King of Prussia and father of Frederick the Great, began a royal stud farm at Trakehner, East Prussia, to supply horses of superior caliber to his cavalry. The breed, which originated from crossing royal hunting stock with high-class Polish Arabians, was established with typical German thoroughness. Heavy training was begun on three- and four-year-olds, at the end of which time a series of tests graded the horses. The best were retained at the stud for breeding, second best went to cavalry officers and third best were sold to private breeders. Those that did not pass were gelded or destroyed. Within a hundred years the Trakehner horse had gained a reputation across Europe for being an outstanding animal, strong and clean-cut, and of fine elegance and swinging stride. And by the end of the nineteenth century they had passed into the hands of small breeders who maintained them with meticulous pride.

During World War II the breed was nearly lost to the Russians. Out of an estimated 10,000 head only 800 managed to escape—across the frozen Baltic, which was breaking up at the time. Many fell through the ice and drowned.

White Wings—an American Albino

Through the years the Trakehner has made a great name for itself in international equestrian events. It has scored some remarkable victories in jumping and dressage events throughout Europe as well as in Olympic competition. Several Trakehners have been imported to Canada, where one ranch is breeding them exclusively. Some are scattered on a less-extensive scale in the United States. Each horse is branded with the double moose antler on the left side.

The Lippizaner, world-famous dressage horse of the Spanish Riding School in Vienna, has also come to America in the last few years. Importations have been large enough so that breeders now have a nucleus for developing and training this royal horse of Austria on our shores.

One thinks of the Lippizaner as being white. Actually he is born black, turns gray as he matures and then silver white with age. Years of intense daily training are required to perfect the advanced maneuvers such as the Levade, Courbette and Capriole. The horse gains its name from the town of Lippiza, where they were bred over four hundred years ago from Spanish stock. There are six family strains, and each horse is branded on the side to indicate his bloodlines.

Among the American importers of the Lippizaner are Mr. and Mrs. Ralph Dreitzler of Kirkland, Washington, who shipped two stallions and four mares to the United States in 1960. Mrs. Dreitzler is one of three women ever to attend Spanish Riding School classes and learn the training and riding methods of this famous dressage school. She, along with other scattered Lippizaner owners, is engaged in training her horses in *haut école* here in America.

The Spanish Riding School in Vienna was formed around 1725 by Emperor Charles VI, a replica of the great Riding Academy of Versailles in France which was ended by the French Revolution. During the seventeenth and eighteenth centuries this type of advanced equipage became the rage of Europe. Most of the royal courts set up elaborate schools for this rigid, almost immobile kind of riding in which the horseman guides his mount through brilliant leaping, stepping and prancing maneuvers on almost invisible cues.

At the end of World War II, as the Russians advanced on Vienna, Colonel Alois Podhajsky, director of the school, shipped his white Lippizaners by rail to western Austria in the hope of being captured by the Americans. At the village of St. Martin he gave himself up to an American general and begged that his breeding stock in Czechoslovakia be saved. The general had little time to be bothered with white horses, but he attended a special show put on by Colonel Podhajsky to convince him of their worth. So impressed was the general, himself an ex-cavalry officer, that he ordered special protection for the horses and sent the convoy to

The smooth-gaited Paso Fino horse from Puerto Rico with rider holding a glass of water and not spilling it

Czechoslovakia to save the remainder. Had it not been for this, the historic Spanish Riding School might have come to its end. The general's name was Patton.

Another interesting horse which is appearing more regularly in the southern United States is the Paso Fino, native of Puerto Rico, with a gait reportedly smoother than the Tennessee Walker. The horse, whose name means fine step, is descended from the original stock of the Spanish horse ranches which were established in the sixteenth and seventeenth centuries. Other blood such as Morgan, Saddle Horse and Arabian has upgraded this most-attractive animal. He is a neat, chunky steed whose tightly coupled body promenades with style and rhythm.

Competitions are held throughout Puerto Rico during the year and all but the very top are eliminated. These then compete in the championship finals each fall in San Juan.

The Paso Fino has spread throughout the West Indies, as far south as Venezuela, and northward to Florida and Texas. It is a breed we will hear more about in coming years.

Another old, old breed which has scattered popularity in the United States is the Norwegian Dun, a short-legged little horse that is quiet and mannerly and sturdy as a bull. He is always dun in color with black trimmings—that is, black mane and tail, black slash down the back and black lower legs, sometimes with cross stripes.

In Scandinavia they are used as work and cart horses that can also be ridden. In the United States they are great fun horses around ranches and farms. They make fine pack horses, willingly pull wagons and stagecoaches for tourists and are wonderful for children to ride in order to gain confidence.

This Fjord-pony may well be the true dun type of horse that prevailed in northern Europe and Russia in prehistoric times. He certainly resembles those pictures drawn by cavemen in France and Spain thousands of years ago.

About the most recent breed of horse to come to America is the Galiceno, a native of the coastal regions of Mexico. Again his origin traces through conquistadors and back to Spain, specifically to the northeast province of Galicia, from whence he gains his name.

But it was principally in Mexico that this sturdy little horse was perfected and maintained as a breed.

And little he is, only 12½ to 13½ hands high and 600 to 650 pounds at maturity. Actually this is pony size, but the Galiceno has the conformation of a small horse, not that of a pony. He is highly intelligent, gentle, easy to handle, a favorite of children who want to learn the gaits of a horse when they are small.

The horse comes in solid colors, predominantly bay, black, sorrel and a few duns. No Paints, Pintos or albinos are eligible for registration. He is an excellent working and contest horse and can jump with the best of the small hunters. Like most small horses, he has smooth, quick gaits.

The Galiceno was first brought to the United States in 1958. Registry and association were begun the following year, and already more than six hundred have been recorded in some twenty states. The horse is ridden with English or Western saddle and has done very well in competition. Caroline Kennedy has one which grazes on the White House lawn.

14.
Ponies

THE PONY WORLD IS GOING DELIGHTFULLY DAFFY. TO explain all that has happened in the last few years, is happening now and apparently will happen in the future would require a book in itself. Old breeds have been refined. New breeds have been created, and new uses found for the pony that no one ever dreamed of before. Changes border on the incredible, but let's cover each breed separately—Shetland, Hackney, Welsh, Connemara, Chincoteague, Pony of the Americas, Americana—and that will tell the story pretty well.

First, a little general information. Ponies are often measured in inches instead of hands, especially when they're short. Originally they came from northern cli-

Shetland ponies chariot racing

mates, particularly the British Isles, which has more varieties of ponies than any other place on earth. The survival of the fittest law eliminated all weaklings in the pony world long ago, so today he is sounder and hardier than the horse. And he usually lives longer, often to thirty years or more.

SHETLAND

The most famous pony in the world is the Shetland. Every child's dream is to own one as a riding pet. The smallest of all ponies, he comes from the barren Shetland Islands north of Scotland. For a thousand years or more he survived on his ability to forage in a land that was almost barren, eating seaweed when there was nothing else. Scarcity of food and the environment cut down his size to the point where he was little more than knee high. Always hardworking, able to survive deep snows and any kind of weather with his thick winter coat, he was gentle, sure-footed, and even if the child fell off, the drop wouldn't be more than a foot or so.

Today there are two kinds of Shetlands: the show type (registered) and the fun type (unregistered). The fun type is the centuries-old, cute little calico. The show type is a miniature Saddle Horse, a flashy high-stepping beauty that performs at pony shows in fine harness and roadster classes, in model and parade classes. This handsome little fellow is groomed and trained to perfection and hauls a glistening little Viceroy buggy that holds the adult driver. The result is all elegance.

There are two height divisions in the show Shetland —forty-six inches to forty-two inches, and forty-two inches and under. Training requires great patience, for although they are easy to handle, the driver must keep the little fellow in true form as well as high style. For the high-knee and-hock action, feet are heavily weighted, as with Saddle Horses.

A decade or so ago everyone jumped into Shetland breeding to make money. It was very simple. All you had to do was get a band of brood mares and a couple of stallions, then sell the young stock as fast as it came along, either privately by advertising or at pony auctions. This kind of breeding was mostly in the fun Shetland, but when the supply caught up with the demand, the only money was in the show pony. Though the field is overpopulated today, an auction of good Shetlands will average $300-$500 a head and as high as $2,500 for superior individuals. The great Captain Topper, generally considered to be the finest Shetland in America, sold at auction for $56,600 in 1960.

HACKNEY

The Hackney pony, with his head of great refinement, body of grace and legs of brilliant action, has long been the gem of the equine world. Originally he came from England, a scaled-down version of the Hackney horse, which the English so superbly developed as a carriage horse by crossing the old Norfolk trotter with the Thoroughbred.

The standard-sized Hackney was recognized everywhere as the pinnacle of harness horses. Canada used them extensively until in recent years road improvement brought autos to remote towns. In America there was no demand for the large size, but we have always loved the Hackney pony, with his regal bearing and fiery eye. He was produced by skillfully crossing the Hackney horse with the best Welsh pony blood, then refining the result through selectivity, as the English do so well.

The only thing that has kept the Hackney pony from putting the other pony breeds out of business in the United States is the fact that he is not good under saddle. His tremendously high action makes him bouncy and stiff to ride, but in harness competition he has no equal. He comes in two sizes: 13 hands and under, and over 13 hands; also two styles: long tail, which requires a full mane, and short-tail, or cob, which requires a tightly braided mane.

Today the Hackney pony is thriving all over the United States, particularly in the Midwest and Iowa, which is a great pony state. Canada has also taken to him. In both countries he's become a favorite among doctors, lawyers, executives and professional people. They seek a pleasant diversion from the tension of their work and thus many have taken up this little demon of the dramatic as a hobby. He is not as big or complicated to manage as a horse, doesn't eat as much, requires much less stable area, care to maintain, and is easier to haul to and from shows.

To take up the reins of a prancing Hackney is no job for the lazy or faint-hearted. It's a real test of skill to tool a bundle of nerves and energy around a show ring and get the most out of the animal while others fly by or bear down on you. The Hackney pony, wherever he goes, is a delight to the eye and picture of elegance.

WELSH

The Welsh Mountain pony, as he is properly called, averages about forty-eight inches in height, comes in solid colors, especially gray, and is very strong for his size. In his native Wales, he carries grown men shepherding in the rough mountain country. Soundness almost always exists in this hardy little animal.

One of the oldest breeds on the British Isles, the Welsh pony carried Britons and their war chariots against Roman legions. Caesar was so impressed with these fiery little steeds that he had many taken back to Rome. The tough Britons never surrendered to the Romans but retreated to the wild mountains of Wales with their little horses and remained there more or less in isolation for nearly two thousand years.

The Welsh pony of today is a beautiful little fellow, hardy, thrifty and sure-footed as a goat. A trace of Arabian shows in him from crosses made years ago, and this has given him refinement and beauty. He is divided into four divisions. Section A ponies are the small, snappy-going show-ring type used mainly for fine harness competition. Section B ponies are somewhat larger and have had Arabian, Thoroughbred, and/or polo-pony blood infused into them. These tend to be Thoroughbred in type and make fine junior hunters and jumpers. Section C includes the heavy-set stock that has draft blood in it, while Section D is for the Welsh Cob,

Photo: Louisa Neilson

Welsh pony jumping

a diminutive fellow considered the best riding and driving pony breed in England.

The ideal Welsh resembles an Arabian in miniature. They are kind, sensible, easily trained animals, and their popularity is steadily growing in America, particularly for English pleasure riding, hunting and showing. He is about the most versatile performer among ponies.

CONNEMARA

This is another great pony coming from the British Isles, specifically from the west of Ireland. The Connemara is good-sized, ranging generally between 13 and 14 hands, and his real forte is hunting and jumping. He comes in solid colors only, all the variations of gray, bay with black points, black, and is a strong fellow capable of taking all kinds of fences and jumps with 140 or more pounds on his back.

In America the Connemara is a junior hunter, and does all the same things from fox hunting to showing that the big Thoroughbred hunter does. He is ideal for those children who are good active riders and are at that awkward age and size when they are too big for a small pony and not really big enough to manage a horse.

CHINCOTEAGUE

Wide is the fame and tall are the tales of the Chincoteague pony, strange remnant of the Virginia coastline islands. This tough little animal has the quality of ponies, for he has withstood coastal storms and hurricanes, annual roundups and auction sales as well as the influx of weaker blood for three hundred years. He inhabits two islands along the northern Virginia coastline—Chincoteague, whence he gains his name, and Assateague, a bleak uninhabited shoal of land where he must fend for himself or die.

The tall tales of his origin? There are many. One says that he is a descendant of some ponies that swam ashore from a wrecked Spanish ship in the sixteenth century. Another says he's the only surviving descendant of *Eohippus* that made it through prehistoric times, but there's absolutely no evidence or logic for this theory. Another says he's descended from the same Choctaw and Chicasaw horses that early Virginian colonists caught and worked and used for quarter-mile racing. These horses originally came from Spanish colonies along the coast of Florida and Georgia. Either the first or the last story is plausible.

In any event the Chincoteague pony was originally solid-colored—bay, black, chestnut—until local residents brought in some Western Pintos as an outcross. Later, Welsh and Shetland blood were both crossed in, and the size, which was originally 14 hands, was reduced to the 12½ to 13½ of today, and the colors are now mixed, ranging from pintos and grays through bay and black.

Because of his rugged environment the Chincoteague pony has mustang endurance and wisdom. Each year the Chincoteague Volunteer Fire Department rounds up the ponies, swims them from the outer island Assateague to the inner island, where a pony auction is held on the last Thursday in July. "Pony penning" it is called, and people come from all over the country to watch and buy if Junior sees one to his liking.

The Chincoteague pony will never win a beauty contest from his flashy relatives the show Shetland and Hackney, but when he is crossed to good Arabian or

Welsh blood the results are excellent. Many people have suggested crossing the best mares to good outside stallions, and in time this will have to be done, for the herd cannot take constant inbreeding. But the rugged Chincoteague will survive as long as his refuge is preserved. Here's hoping that he remains well guarded so our children can see and feel this fragment of American heritage.

PONY OF THE AMERICAS

"If you can have a Quarter Horse," cried the boy to his father, "why can't I have a Quarter pony?" "Because there's no such thing." "Well, they should have one!" the boy shouted, on the verge of tears. "I want to do with my pony what you do with your horse."

After this scene had occurred with most men who had Quarter Horses and sons, someone hit upon the bright idea of creating a pony to match Junior's dreams. When Dad competed with his Quarter Horse, Junior could compete with his Quarter pony. What kind would he like the best? Why, an Appaloosa, naturally!

And so it happened. By crossing a small Appaloosa stallion to a Welsh or Shetland, the Pony of the Americas was created. The breed, dubbed POA, is still being perfected, but it's well on its way. Height is between forty-six and fifty-two inches at maturity. The idea is to have a pony of stock-horse conformation small enough for a child to ride yet large enough for a man to break and train. A registry, started in 1954, already covers forty states. A pony of any breed or combination of breeds that has stock-horse type and Appaloosa coloring may be registered. Basically, he's a using pony and in the show ring is penalized for high action and extreme refinement. Show classes are patterned after Dad's halter, cutting, and roping events. Instead of cutting or roping steers or calves, the kids use goats.

But before you run out and buy a POA you'd better save a lot of pennies, for they're about the hottest hunk of horseflesh going at the moment. Plenty of good, well-trained stock horses sell for under $1,000 at auctions, but a green-broke POA stallion will nearly always fetch $1,500, and good ones $3,000 to $5,000 with no trouble.

An enterprising youngster who knows the knack of handling horses could easily put himself through college by raising and training a couple of POA's. With a herd of them he wouldn't have to bother going.

AMERICANA

Enter another new addition to the pony world—the Americana. He's a cross between registered Hackney and registered Shetland. Why create this new breed? For one thing, the Hackney has always been a large pony and the market wanted something smaller. Shetland breeders refined their old-fashioned pony into a high-stepping dandy, but he still did not have the overall elegance of the Hackney. When the Shetland market began to tighten up, someone came up with the idea of crossing the Hackney and the Shetland to create a new breed—the Americana.

A national organization was formed, a registry begun and much publicity poured out before the first Americana foal appeared. The standard says that the Americana must be forty-six inches or under. Those over this height can be used for breeding only. The Americana is to be a beautiful animal with a highly refined head, eye and ear, and must possess top conformation while having high action. The size is kept down mainly through the mares.

Some say the breed was started to supply an outlet for registered Shetlands, and this may well be the case. There has been increased activity, but mainly among the breeders themselves. Each Shetland breeder bought a good Hackney stallion or two, and the Hackney people acquired a few head of Shetland mares to be ready just in case the Americana went over big. The first foals are now appearing and it will be interesting to see what happens to this new show-pony breed. The Hackney, Shetland and Welsh are very similar as fine-harness ponies and the question remains whether the Americana can be made distinctive enough to survive.

One of the exciting new uses for the pony is as a racing trotter. Fitted out like a Standardbred, he has taken to the track in full force and started a whirlwind of enthusiasm.

Pony roadster classes have always been popular. In these the pony performs at an animated trot, pulling a sulky and driver just as a Standardbred. As inevitably happened, someone challenged someone else to a trotting race, and now a whole new world is growing up around the racing pony. Shetlands and Welshes are generally used, many registered, the majority grades and crosses.

State associations have sprung up from Maine to Florida and across the country to California. The United States Pony Trotting Association has set up rules and sanctions meets. Because of the variety of events this is a real family sport. There are various types of classified trots for Dad and son, ladies' races for Mom, children's races and free-for-alls for those who think they're really good. Meets are held at minor tracks with purses ranging from $100 to $300. Distances are one-quarter and one-half mile.

At this point the sport is strictly amateur, but as it grows and the purses get bigger, professionals will inevitably jump in. One day we may see Shetlands featured in the first race at Yonkers or elsewhere.

CHARIOT RACING

Another fantastic offshoot of the pony world is chariot racing. This sport, which is growing by leaps and bounds in the Pacific Northwest and Midwest, may someday prove to be one of our hottest amateur sports.

The Chariot Racing World Championships are held annually in Spokane, Washington, and teams come from many parts of the country to compete. Capacity crowds are attracted at fairs where stakes money runs as high as $3,000 per meet. Ponies must be fifty inches or under. For a time they were raced according to height brackets, but it turned out that the bigger ponies didn't always have the added speed that was expected, so a speed-classification system is now used.

Rigid rules are applied to the health of the ponies and condition of chariot and harness. No driver is allowed to race without first passing a driver's test and having his equipment checked. After all requirements are passed, he is issued a license good for one year. The following year he must pass the same requirements again. Chariot racing is done with a two-pony hitch, and anything that can run is used. It's not the gory free-for-all of Roman charioteers in the old Circus Maximus, but it's an exciting sport to viewers as well as participants.

Other types of pony racing include Chuck Wagon racing, Relay racing, Six-up-Hitch, and flat racing under saddle, which is just beginning. Distances are 110, 220, 330 and 440 yards, with standards based on Quarter Horse racing rules.

The pony world has changed a lot in the last ten years, and it promises to change considerably more in the next ten.

15.
Polo

FOR MANY YEARS PEOPLE HAVE BEEN SAYING THAT POLO died with World War II. When the U.S. Cavalry was mechanized, over one thousand army polo players were lost. When army Remount Stations, which kept Thoroughbred stallions available for light-horse breeders, were closed, a prime source of polo ponies was lost. During the 1930's, around seven hundred students received polo instruction annually from army officers at twenty ROTC colleges and universities throughout the country. At the end of World War II, two-thirds of the players and most of the mounts were out of the game forever. It looked as though the critics were right. The Golden Age of polo, when forty thousand cheered the great international matches on Long Island, had passed into oblivion.

But such was not the case. Polo is a magnificent active game that can be played by men up to sixty years of age. The stars reach their peak usually in the late thirties and early forties. It is a glamorous game, a challenging game that demands both physical and mental dexterity. Besides exercise and timing it requires self-control and quick decisions followed by instant action, qualities of high-caliber men, which is why the American and British armies always encouraged polo playing by the military and why polo would not die. Slowly but persistently it came back.

Out of the eighty-eight clubs which are now members of the United States Polo Association, seventy-three have joined since 1946. Several colleges have rejuvenated polo on their athletic curriculum—Cornell, Georgetown, Harvard, Princeton, Stanford, University of Virginia, and Yale along with Culver and Valley Forge Military Academy.

Polo is getting progressively stronger because its progenitors have been foresighted enough to alter the game so that it meets the changing times. Arena polo and shorter fields now make it possible to play the game with only one pony per man whereas three used to be and still is the absolute minimum for high-goal tournaments on the regulation 160-by-300-yard field. College teams and new groups now play with three men instead

Arabian Costume Class winner

Training for a long distance endurance ride

of four. A special beginner's polo kit supplies a saddle, two mallets, a dozen balls, polo helmet, bridle, bit, spurs and whip for under $200. Figure another $500 to $1,500 for a pony; financially the game is about the same as campaigning a show horse or jumper. And if you want real exercise, just try eight 7½-minute chukkers of polo.

More polo clubs are concentrated in the western Pennsylvania-Ohio area and the Maryland-Virginia area than in any other section of the country. Playing on an economic scale geared to a moderate income, the clubs are organized into leagues similar to bowling and are handicapped according to ability. The Maryland-Virginia Polo League boasts ten clubs which have one or more teams. They hold interleague as well as invitational tournaments with other teams around the country.

Santa Barbara has become a great polo center on the West Coast, as has Palm Springs. Both have ultraplush facilities, and on weekends builders, realtors and doctors in private planes fly in for a practice game or big tournament. There may not be the perfection of the old days, but every match is a hard-fought duel and the crowds are coming back. In Florida over sixty-two thousand fans turned out for a sixteen-Sunday schedule to watch big league polo. To get the people in, the promoters staged beauty contests, sky-diving shows, sports-car rallies, band concerts, benefit games with celebrities

128

Trail riding

and an egg-rolling contest on Easter Sunday, and it worked.

Potentially polo has always been a great spectator sport because of its reckless, charging, hard-riding tactics. This ancient Persian game which traces back to the tenth century spread to Tibet, China and even Japan before British army officers picked the game up in the Manipur province of India and brought it to the Occidental world. The game is still played extensively in England and on the Continent. In our hemisphere the South Americans are outstanding players. It is a national sport in Argentina and the cream of the polo ponies generally come from there.

American polo was first played in New York City in 1876 on Texas cow ponies. When polo became established here it was played on almost any fast, active pony. Then someone noticed that in contests between evenly matched teams the men with the best ponies won, so polo players began breeding special mounts. An attempt to standardize the height at 14½ hands failed because

Roping

Pleasure riding

breeders couldn't consistently produce a hardy, fast, intelligent and sound pony with this restriction. Speed and great endurance were basic requirements, so the Thoroughbred naturally came into play. Size was ignored, and today a polo mount is often a horse of 16 hands, but still called a pony. Generally he is half-Thoroughbred or more.

A polo pony should be close-coupled and, when standing, look square; that is, his height should be about the same as his length. In motion he must be agile and quick as a ballet dancer. Usually he has a long thin neck and this is what allows him to turn so quickly. The neck spins after the ball and the body follows. Rearward, he resembles a Quarter Horse, heavily muscled buttocks, hocks neatly let down and well under him, for he pivots constantly with and on his hind quarters, and he must have the strength to burst instantly from a standstill into a gallop. Forelegs are strong and supple. Quality stands out. Tails of polo ponies are bound to keep them out of the way. Cannon bones are wrapped for protection. The horse must not only learn to follow the ball instinctively but to take

Shark Sun—Dressage exhibition stallion

Surf—champ trail-riding Arabian

the bodily punishment that comes from charging opponents, blocking them and riding them out. It requires about two and a half years of training to make a polo pony good.

To encourage more interest in polo, the U.S. Polo Association has sponsored polo schools in both the East and West. At these clinics young people learn the proper way of approaching and stroking the ball, the various shots, and defensive and offensive playing. Television and the newspapers have given the sport a bigger play lately and this has increased spectator interest. But the future of polo is most assured by colleges that have taken up the game again. From their ranks will come the Tommy Hitchcocks and the Cecil Smiths of tomorrow, the Pan-American and Olympic competitors and those low-goal players who love the excitement of hard riding and that tingling thrill when the mallet cleanly meets the ball and drives it home for a goal. By them will this great game and its traditions be upheld.

16.

The horse
in competition

THE EARLIEST RECORD OF COMPETING WITH HORSES DATES
back to the first Olympic Games held in the eighth century B.C. by the Greeks, who were great horse lovers and
masters in the art of horsemanship. The Greeks always
rode bareback and, oddly, this is the only classification
of competitive riding for which there is nothing today.
Bareback bronc riding might be so considered, but the
purpose is not cooperation between horse and man,
rather the lack of it, and for a ten-second interval at
most. The Greeks might have laughed at this but they
wouldn't have laughed at the amazing variety of ways
and means we have found to compete with horses.

They fall roughly into four catagories: horse shows,
trail rides, parades and rodeos.

133

The horse show was inherited from the eighteenth-century agricultural shows and horse fairs of England. Our first horse shows in the modern sense were at Litchfield, Connecticut, in 1841 and Upperville, Virginia, in 1855, both of which are still thriving. In 1833 the first National Horse Show was held in New York City's old Madison Square Garden and furnished great impetus to other groups. At that time harness horses of various types comprised the major portion of the show. Riding horses played a rather minor role while hunters and jumpers were way-out oddities and Western classes non-existent. Today the reverse of this is true.

The large modern horse show has many divisions. In Equitation classes, popular for youngsters under eighteen, the amateur rider is judged on ability to handle the horse, change gaits, maintain a proper seat, balance, and good hands. In the hunter Equitation classes knockdowns do not count unless they are the fault of the rider, though knocking down every fence doesn't help the score.

In the hunter division, so popular in the East, horses simulate fox-hunting conditions over either an outside course or jumps within the show ring. Most of these horses are three-quarters, seven-eighths or straight Thoroughbred. They are judged usually 60 percent on performance and 40 percent on conformation. Sometimes appointments are considered, which means the proper hunting attire and tack.

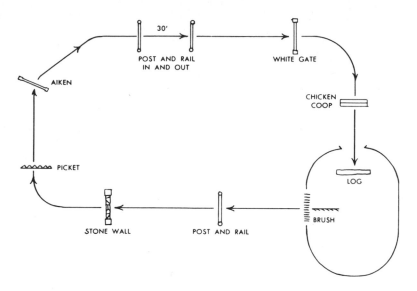

A typical outside course for Hunters. Heights and spacings are modified for Junior Hunters and ponies.

Jumping is one of the most exciting spectator events at a horse show. Any kind of horse that can leap is used, and some mighty strange-looking ones saved from the glue factory have gone on to become champions. Jumping is a real art. The big stakes are not necessarily won by the best horse but usually by the best-ridden horse. Good riders count the number of strides between

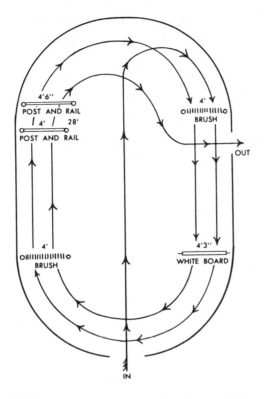

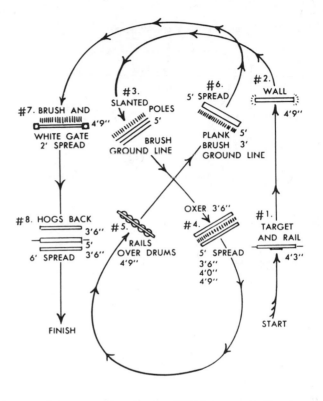

A typical course for Working Hunter, Corinthian. In this class riders are amateurs who are members of a Recognized or Registered Hunt and must perform in full hunting attire.

A typical Puissance jumping course. The object is to test the horse's ability to jump large obstacles. All barriers except the first must be a minimum of four feet six inches. In the event of a tie there are compulsory jump-offs over a reduced number of obstacles which have been raised and/or increased in width.

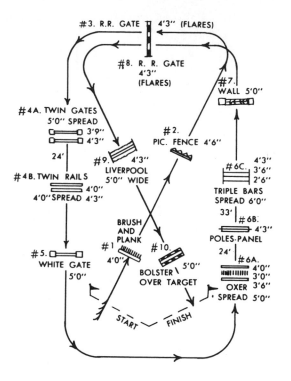

#3. R.R. GATE 4'3" (FLARES)

#8. R. R. GATE 4'3" (FLARES)

#7. WALL 5'0"

#4A. TWIN GATES 5'0" SPREAD
3'9"
4'3"
24'

#2. PIC. FENCE 4'6"

#9. 4'3"
LIVERPOOL 5'0" WIDE

#6C. 4'3"
3'6"
2'6"

#4B. TWIN RAILS
4'0"
4'0" SPREAD 4'3"

TRIPLE BARS SPREAD 6'0"
33'
#6B.
4'3"
POLES-PANEL
24'
#6A.

BRUSH AND PLANK

#1
4'0"

#10.

#5.
WHITE GATE 5'0"

BOLSTER OVER TARGET

5'0"

OXER 3'6"
SPREAD 5'0"
4'0"
3'0"

START FINISH

A typical Open Jumper Stake with a $500 or $1,000 purse

jumps, keep their mounts paced as evenly as possible and know their horse's strong points and weaknesses. The Puissance class is always the hair-raiser because here horse and rider face the highest and most difficult jumps. International jumping is thrilling also, and no one can watch it without pedaling his feet or raising his shoulders to help the horse over the barriers.

In 1961 the American Horse Shows Association, founded in 1917 as the ruling body of the sport, sanctioned over five hundred shows which awarded more than $1,500,000 in prize money. This is only a fraction of the shows and of the money actually given away. None of the breed shows or Quarter Horse shows are included in this.

There are all kinds of horse shows being held across the country, ranging from the half-day gymkhana to shows of national importance which last a week or more. Among the great outdoor events might be included the Devon Horse Show and Country Fair, Ox Ridge, Fairfield County Hunt Club, Detroit, Del Mar, Piping Rock and Lexington. Some of the great indoor winter shows are the American Royal at Kansas City, the Washington International, the Pennsylvania National at Harrisburg, the National at New York, and the Royal Winter Fair in Toronto. The last four all feature international jumping teams from England, Canada, Mexico, Germany, Brazil, Argentina, Venezuela, Chile, Ireland, Spain, France and the United States.

Horse shows serve many purposes. Beyond the thrill of professionals vying for the big-money stakes, breeders have the opportunity to show off their stock and let it bear the stern test of competition. Showing is also a source of great pleasure for the amateur horse owner whether he is commercially inclined or not. Beyond being fun and healthful it teaches young people the need for self-discipline and training in order to win, also how to lose gracefully. For the skillful adult horseman it can provide the pinnacle of achievement. For the person who has loved and lived with horses throughout a lifetime to win in a fifty-year-and-over class provides a great personal satisfaction.

Ribbons are awarded to winners at the conclusion of each class. This varies from four to eight placements. A trophy, either permanent or rotating, is generally awarded to the first-place winner and ribbons pinned to the bridle of each winning horse. The color indicates the position as follows:

Blue	First
Red	Second
Yellow	Third
White	Fourth
Pink	Fifth
Green	Sixth
Purple	Seventh
Brown	Eighth

There are also Championship ribbons colored as follows:

Blue, red, yellow and white   Grand Champion

Red, yellow, white and pink   Reserve Grand Champion

Blue, red and yellow   Champion

Red, yellow and white   Reserve Champion

Three important trends have appeared in horse shows of the past few years: an increased interest in events leading to international competitions like the Olympic and Pan-American games; greater emphasis on children's classes; and tremendous increase in all events of the Western division.

When the U.S. Army Cavalry was dissolved in 1948 our country was left without representation in international equestrian competition. In 1950 the United States Equestrian Team was organized to fill the gap, and it has done a great job. At first only men were allowed on the team, but this rule has been lifted and the result has been that girls are training ardently to pass the try-outs, which qualify them to represent our country at the great international horse shows and jumping competitions around the world.

As for the children, most shows now give their classes prominent places in the program, and many shows are entirely devoted to juniors. And why not, for what better foundation is there for maintaining the tradition of fine horses and horsemanship than the young people?

Western riding? That's been on the rampage for a decade now. During that time many new breed shows have appeared for the Quarter Horse, the Appaloosa, the Arabian, and now the Pinto and others. These breed shows include all kinds of events from Western pleasure, cutting and model classes to barrel-racing, jumping, costume and flat-racing events.

Beyond that, the Western stock horse has changed the composition of nearly every show in the country. In the East, where English-style riding was always the vogue, where equitation, hunting, jumping and gaited classes made up the show program, the Western division now often comprises 50 percent of the classes or more.

The cutting horse in action is a fascinating animal to watch. He works with a loose rein and receives almost no guidance from the rider, yet maintains a constant advantage over the cow, drifting with it, heading it off and pivoting with explosive suddenness to block off a thrust back to the herd.

Rules for this event are set up by the National Cutting Horse Association, and last year total prize money for this single event amounted to more than $500,000. There are an estimated five thousand active cutting horses in the United States, and an outstanding one is a moneymaker selling as high as $30,000, though they almost never come up for sale. When you realize that the top fifty cutting horses working professionally today are all so closely matched that the slightest fault amounts to elimination, then the quality of the horse becomes apparent. Training the cutting horse means training one of the greatest of all horses. There are men who spend their lives doing only this, and it is a profitable profession.

Roping is another phase of Western competition that has grown tremendously in the last few years. The best ropers are professionals who follow the rodeo circuit, like Dean Oliver, who annually earns around $25,000 or better in this event. Most horse shows with Western divisions have roping events now and even Junior can have a throw. Roping horses are highly skilled animals trained to stop the moment the rope falls over the calf's neck, then back-pedal to throw the calf and maintain a taut rope until the tie is completed.

Reining is another interesting phase of Western competition. Originally the idea was to show the maneuverability of the horse and in so doing an intricate pattern has evolved. Reining horses turn at the slightest signal, so sharply that the average rider often goes flying off into space unless he's prepared. They turn 180 degrees on their hocks, pivot 90 degrees right and left and are among the most maneuverable horses in the world.

Barrel racing has become a popular ladies sport all over the country. In 1962 it appeared at the National Horse Show in Madison Square Garden for the first

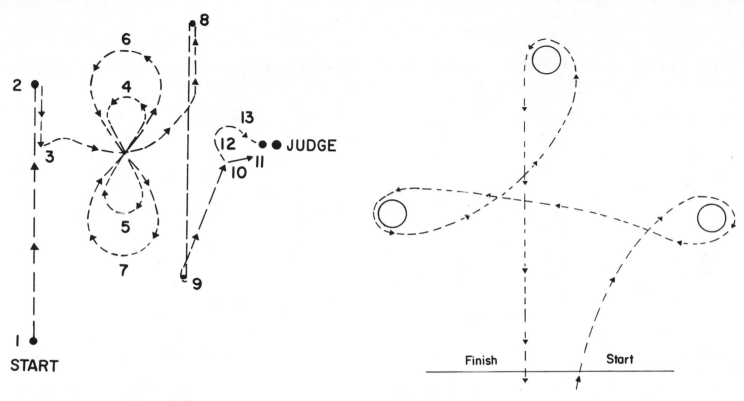

START

Reining Pattern—ridden as follows:
  1 to 2—Run at full speed
  2—Stop and back
  3—Settle horse for 10 seconds
  4 and 5—Ride small figure eight. Judge's instruction either
        to right or left
  6 and 7—Ride large figure eight
  8—Left roll back over hocks
  9—Right roll back over hocks
  10—Stop
  11—Pivot right
  12—Pivot left
  13—Walk to judge and stop for inspection until dismissed

Barrel racing pattern

time, and today a show of any size includes this event, which is run against time. Prize money grows larger annually. A girl can win $3,000 to $5,000 a year, an indication why good barrel-racing horses are expensive. To train one the rider begins by walking the horse around the three barrels in racing pattern, later trots and lopes, and finally races him full speed over and over. Barrel-racing horses grow to love the sport so much that they get all steamed up the moment they see a barrel anywhere. The secret to speed is training the horse to cut closely around the barrels without knocking them over. Contests are won and lost in the turns. Winning times are always under twenty seconds. Each year a National Champion and stakes and regional champions are crowned on a point-per-dollar-won system.

Western Pleasure Horse and Stock Seat Equitation classes are usually crowded with entries. In these two events the true Western horse and his rider come to the fore. In the Pleasure class the horse is judged—60 percent on performance and manners, 30 percent on type, conformation, quality and substance and 10 percent on appointments, which again include proper tack and riding attire. In the Equitation class the rider is judged on his manners, posture and method of handling his horse. It's important to know all the rules of performance and details of dress, for in large classes a judge must split hairs to choose the winners. Horses are shown at walk, jog and lope both ways of the ring, and must always be on the proper lead.

The Western Trail Horse class is another challenging event where performance is over and through obstacles, particularly opening, passing through and closing a gate, stepping over logs and backing through narrow openings. Horses are shown at walk, jog and lope, with special emphasis on the walk. A good trail horse should be a good pleasure horse with the ability to navigate obstacles encountered in trail riding.

Halter, or Model, classes—both are the same except that different breeds use different terminology—often comprise a third of a show nowadays. Quarter Horse people in particular go in heavily for this because a Quarter Horse champion must have gained the required points at halter as well as working classes. This proves that he has both conformation and ability. Showing a horse properly in a halter class is not as simple as it looks. The best handler can't make a poor horse win, but he can certainly help a good one show his best. Grooming and conditioning are of the utmost importance, also keeping the horse mannerly while showing in the ring. There is nothing a judge dislikes more than to have a horse kick at him as he walks down the line behind them. There is no excuse for this. The owner should take the time to break his horse of such a habit.

Two of the most popular competitions developed in recent years have been the Parade and Costume classes.

The parade horse is a beautiful, stylish animal displaying refinement and personality. Horse and rider together must present eye-appeal. Unless the class is restricted, any type of horse may be used provided he can show at the two required gaits: the animated, graceful walk and the parade gait, a high-prancing trot. The horse is faulted for excessive speed, extreme position of tail, bad manners, switching tail, exaggerated opening of mouth, hard mouth, lugging on bridle and fighting bit, halting or hesitating, zigzagging or sidewise movement, or carrying sour ears. These classes are most beautiful because the horse wears an elaborate silver saddle with Mexican parade trappings and the rider wears the colorful attire of the Old West of either American, Mexican or Spanish origin—fancy cowboy suit, hat and boots, spurs, guns and serapes, etc. Judging is 75 percent on performance, manners and conformation of horse and 25 percent on appointments of horse and rider.

Fun and colorful costume classes come in wide variety from Gay Nineties to Wild West. Almost every breed has one. The Appaloosas are particularly beautiful and authentically prepared to represent the Nez Percé Indian. Fine-harness horse and pony groups also have elaborate costume classes.

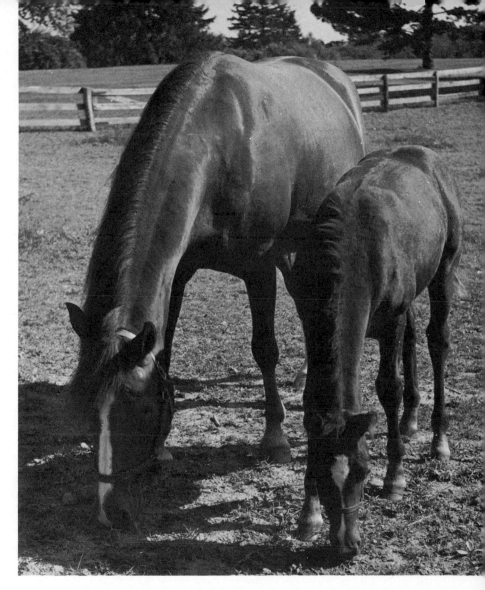

In recent years one of the great areas for competing with the horse has been trail riding. Contests of 50- and 100-mile length are being held in almost every state across the country, and the people who compete in them probably love to ride their horses in the great outdoors, over mountains, through valleys, across rivers and streams, through deep forests and along the ocean's shore more than any other group.

It takes considerable conditioning of both horse and rider to prepare for an endurance ride. Generally a 100-mile ride is spread over three days, 40, 30 and 30. Judges are hidden along the route to make certain participants abide by the rules, and veterinarians at stopovers check every phase of the horses' condition. A horse is not permitted to continue if at any point he is found to be unsound or exhausted.

The real endurance rides, like the 100-mile one-day Tevis Cup ride from Lake Tahoe to Auburn, California, are fantastic tests of a horse's and rider's capacities. On this particular ride competitors climb a total of 9,500 feet and descend a total of 15,250 feet. The temperature is 45 degrees when they start in darkness at 5 A.M. They begin an ascent through stands of Ponderosa pine to mountain meadows flanked by the Olympic ski lifts of Squaw Valley. The path climbs 2,000 feet to snow-covered Emigrant Pass, then follows the gold miners' trail of the Forty-Niners down the Sierra Nevada Divide and along a stony ridge with flanking valleys 2,000 feet below. In spots the horses must climb over sheets of rock for several hundred yards, but the lava base is soft enough to keep them from slipping. All the while the scenery is breathtaking, among the most beautiful in the world. A few more miles of lumber roads, an hour's stop for breakfast and then the vets move in.

Each horse's pulse, respiration, temperature and condition are recorded immediately upon arrival, and again an hour later. Two or three horses end here because of poor conditioning, but for the majority the recovery rate is satisfactory, so horse and rider push on to the famous Last Chance Mine. Streams are forded, and climbing out of steep canyons requires riders to rest their horses a minute every 200 or 300 yards so the animals can catch their breaths. On to the Deadwood Mine, through the cemetery of its ghost town, then down into El Dorado Canyon, the thermometer now in the 90's, and on through Michigan Bluff, with its old stone store and few scattered houses where Leland Stanford got his financial start as a storekeeper during the Gold Rush.

A second hour's stop, more tests, a bite to eat. By this time more than sixty miles have been covered—the most rugged part of the journey—but a long distance still remains, most of it to be ridden by moonlight. Some mounts cannot continue, but the strong, sound horses are off again, weaving 2,000 feet down to Volcano

Canyon and on through the Robie timber lands, eventually ending up another 2,000 feet below at the American River, along whose banks gold was found in 1849. A third stop for an hour. More dropouts, especially from high blood pressure. Everyone is tired, but those who can, push on along the trail beside the river, past one old mining camp after another; and the gravel bars where gold was panned a hundred years before by hordes of men glisten silently in the moonlight. Ninety-four miles out the trail crosses the first tarred road, continues over a concrete railroad bridge and climbs slowly to the city limits of Auburn. At the edge of town another fifteen-minute veterinary check, then on in through the streets to the finish line at the Fair Grounds.

The first horse over is not necessarily the winner. Instead, it's the soundest horse to finish within an hour after the first horse. This keeps riders from pushing their mounts excessively. The winner generally completes the 100 miles in less than fourteen hours, thus averaging better than seven miles an hour over some of the roughest terrain in the world. Checkups the next morning usually decide the winner. Lame horses are penalized, heart murmurs too, as are excessively high temperatures or pulse rates en route or afterward. To win the Tevis Cup is a supreme accomplishment. If you come off with a belt buckle, which signifies that you completed the ride within twenty-four hours, it's a proud possession, and the memory of the ride lingers as

an unforgettable experience, just as all great trail rides do.

Participating in parades is another interesting phase of the horse world. Included are Sheriff's Posse groups, riding clubs and drill teams, particularly numerous in the South and West, where brilliant precision maneuvers are performed. It takes hours of practice, but there is the fun of working in a group with your horse and afterward having a cookout or barbecue. The big reward is to take part in great parades across the country, like the annual Rose Bowl parade and the Parada del Sol in Arizona, even the Inaugural Parade in Washington. Individuals and horses are usually invited to enter these. Horses must be mannerly around crowds and unafraid of noisy bands. Riders must dress colorfully and have their mounts decked out to perfection. Showy silver-mounted tack is used. Parades are generally judged and prizes awarded to outstanding groups and individuals.

The last phase of horse competition is the rodeo. Though in many events it is the rider and not the horse that competes, still everyone is centered around or uses the horse in some capacity. Participants are either professionals who follow the rodeo circuit for a livelihood or enthusiastic amateurs who test their luck and skill on weekends. For the professionals it's a bone-cracking way of earning a living, and the smart ones retire early to become producers supplying bucking horses and wild Brahma bulls that keep their buddies bouncing.

Amateur rodeos are staged somewhere in the West and Southwest almost every weekend of the year. Beyond the bucking bronco, bull-riding, and dogging events are roping, cutting, reining, team roping (called heading and tailing) and barrel racing. In fact, all types of Western classes. College rodeos have also become popular among girls and boys at universities.

Even youngsters have rodeos. Back in 1932 the town of Florence, Arizona, badly needed money for its school milk fund. A local cattleman suggested to the PTA that a rodeo for junior contestants be held in which his son and other youngsters could participate. From that small beginning have grown the hundreds of junior rodeos now produced annually in the United States. The American Junior Rodeo Association holds elaborate finals in Sweetwater, Texas, every year with junior world championship titles at stake. Barrel racing, roping, bull and bareback bronc riding are only a small part of the huge program at which a new two-horse trailer, thirty-odd hand-tooled championship saddles, sixty gold-and-silver trophy buckles and a roping-school award are part of the more than $5,000 worth of prizes. AJRA-approved junior rodeos are held throughout the country, and almost every state is represented at the junior Finals.

There are many wonderful as well as profitable ways of competing in the horse world, and there are also some basic rules that apply everywhere.

Dress is important. Be neat, not flashy, and wear what the rules call for. Judges are very strict on this. Improper attitre annoys them as much as anything no matter what the type of riding. Get an American Horse Shows Association rule book. This will tell you not only how to dress but give the requirements of each class for all English-type shows and many Western events.

Another thing: do your training outside the ring or arena, never in it. You'll only make a fool of yourself and lose spectator regard. If your horse cuts up on a particular day and you can't control him, ride out of the ring and give the others a break. An unruly horse will never place and he's a danger to the other contestants.

Be a good loser as well as a modest winner. Don't whine over a judge's decision. There's nothing improper in seeking him out later and asking the reasons for his decision. Don't do it with a know-it-all attitude. Ask him what you did wrong and how you can improve the next time out.

Remember that no one in history ever won all the time. Practice makes perfect, and perfection is never denied.

17.
Basic riding

THERE IS A SAYING THAT YOU'RE NEVER TOO YOUNG NOR too old to learn to ride a horse. No doubt that the younger you start the better, but you can learn at any age. If you have never done it and would like to become engaged in a year-around sport that offers endless variety, pleasant associates, as well as rewarding solitary rambles, then horseback riding should be considered.

Don't get the impression that there's nothing to it, that the first time out you ride blithely away. You're apt to run into complications. The horse may be more than you can manage, in which case the ride can border on a nightmare and you may end up too frightened to try again. The horse may do something simple with which you in your inexperience cannot cope. He may shy, he may not want to leave the stable alone, he may leave docilely and become a roaring bronco the moment you turn for home, or he may persist in trotting all the time and nearly bouncing the teeth out of your head if you don't know how to post. You will not gain much experience in riding if these or other unfamiliar incidents occur.

Riding may be begun in three ways: borrow a friend's horse, rent one from a public stable, or buy your own. This last is not advisable in the beginning, and if you have no friend who owns a horse, don't be discouraged. He probably wouldn't let you borrow it anyway. Why? Because he doesn't want to find dirty tack every time he goes to use it; he doesn't want his horse getting bad habits; and, above all, because he doesn't want to be sued if you accidentally fall off. Legal precedent favors the claimant. So you will probably be forced to the nearest stable to rent a horse, but don't be discouraged because you will meet other beginners. Also, you can take private or group instruction, which is by far the best way to learn. Private lessons cost between $5 and $10 an hour, group lessons less, but you don't learn as fast. Children and timid grownups should definitely take private instruction at the start.

It's important to be careful around horses, but not afraid of them. Most accidents are due to neglect, carelessness or lack of knowledge on the horseman's part.

In the beginning be sure to ask for a calm horse. You can learn much quicker and gain confidence too. The spirited steed can come later. Also, it's better to practice around the stable ring or corral for several sessions before taking off on your own. This will familiarize you with the basics as well as with two or three different mounts.

As for clothes, the beginner ought to buy a pair of ready-made washable jodhpurs ($9.95 and up) if he or she is going to ride with an English saddle. With these should be worn jodhpur boots ($6.95 and up) or at least a pair of stout shoes. Sneakers and loafers are too limber and can be dangerous. If you ride Western, you can get by with blue jeans and Western boots if you have them. Wear long underwear under the blue jeans no matter what the season, otherwise you may end up with raw knees and calves. A good windbreaker will take the place of a riding jacket at first. Ladies should wear light leather gloves.

Obviously the first decision you make is the type of saddle and bridle to use. The stable boy or instructor will ask what you want. There are three basic seats in riding, each with a different type of saddle and bridle. The hunter seat requires a saddle with a rather high cantle (rear), knee pads for jumping, and a snaffle bridle. The saddle seat, used for three- and five-gaited horses, requires a saddle with a relatively flat cantle and set farther back on the horse's back, and a double bridle,

Mounting English style: first step

Mounting English style: second step

Mounting English style: mount completed

that is, with a curb bit and a small snaffle bit, consequently four reins instead of the usual two. The Western seat requires the Western, or stock, saddle, which has an extremely deep seat and Western bridle or hackamore.

Many feel more secure in a Western saddle because they can grab the horn and hang on. That should not be your reason for choosing it. Your choice of tack should depend on the type of riding you're going to do and the locale of the country you're in. You don't jump in a Western saddle and you couldn't barrel race very well in an English saddle. In the beginning you should try all three and be familiar with the feel of each one. Don't decide right away, because too much depends on your decision—the clothes you wear, the type of horse you may someday own and the show classes you may someday enter. At this stage the important thing is to learn correct riding habits and practice them over and over until they're second nature.

That doesn't mean using a mounting block to get into the saddle. It means mounting properly under your own power. For the first few times, ask someone to hold the bridle of the horse to make sure he stands still. This way you won't be nervous about the horse bolting out from under you and can concentrate on mounting properly.

Mounting and dismounting are done from the left, or near, side of the horse. Stand by the horse's left shoulder, gather the reins in the left hand tight enough so there is no slack. Throw the bight, or loose end, over to the other side, out of the way, and grab a handful of mane just above the withers where the front, or pommel, of the saddle rests. If the mane is clipped, put your hand on the pommel and plan to pull on that instead. Now raise your left foot and place it in the stirrup with the right hand. Reach up with the right hand and seize the cantle of the saddle, give a skip and a hop off the right foot, pull with both hands and you're up. Don't pause vertically but swing the right leg over the horse's rump and settle into the saddle and immediately slip the right foot into its stirrup. There, you're up and on!

As you will soon learn, the secret of mounting is to combine the spring off the right foot with the pull of both arms. It's only a matter of timing and practice. Once you're in the saddle you can slip your foot into the stirrup by feeling for it with your toe. Don't bend over and try to put it in with your hand. This leaves you completely out of balance and almost helpless in the event that the horse begins to move.

Mounting English and Western are practically the same except that Western people tend to face the saddle, whereas the English style is to stand ahead of the saddle and face the rear, then spin into the skip-and-hop movement.

Also, in mounting Western, the right hand is placed

Mounting Western style: first step

Photo: Dick Spohn

Mounting Western style: second step

Photo: Dick Spohn

Mounting Western style: mount completed

front on the saddle horn instead of rear on the cantle. When you hop off your right foot, the pull of your right arm automatically swings you over the horse's back and into the saddle, whereas with the English you have to make the twist.

Since you're now in the saddle, you're ready to ride, but before you start let's dismount and try it again. This will teach you how to get off a horse and improve your mounting.

To dismount Western style is the exact reverse of mounting. English style is a little different. You swing over to the left side of the horse and stand with both legs parallel, but with the left foot still in the stirrup. Place your left hand on the pommel, right hand on the cantle, shift your weight to your arms enough to free your left foot and then let yourself slide lightly to the ground.

No matter which type of saddle you're seated in, sit up straight, with head high and eyes forward. *Don't look down,* because this will tend to throw your posture forward and out of balance. No need to sit ramrod straight but comfortably erect, with elbows close to sides and hands over the withers, holding the reins not tautly but firmly so you have contact with the horse's mouth. The ball of the foot rests in the stirrup, heels down, ankles rolled so the toes point out slightly.

Before mounting, stirrups must be adjusted to suit your legs. The simplest way to do this is to take in or let out the stirrup leather until it is approximately arm length. Stirrups should be long enough so your knees are slightly bent. This helps to clear the saddle when posting to the trot. Western stirrups are worn longer, with only a slight leg bend.

Remember the three gaits—walk, trot and canter on an English saddle, and walk, jog and lope on a Western.

First will be the walk. Once in the saddle, get your wits about you. Use both hands on the reins at the start. If you have a snaffle bridle (that means one rein in each hand that runs under the little finger, through the palm and out the top of the hand between thumb and forefinger with the bight falling between the hands, which are held about four inches apart and over the withers) *sit up straight with eyes ahead.*

In Western riding there are two ways of holding the reins: standard and California. By far the majority use the standard grip, which is simply laying the reins in the left palm and closing on them with thumb and forefinger and letting the slack fall from the back of the hand. No fingers between the reins—this is the rule. In the California grip the hand is held in a fist and the reins come from the underside, out the top by the thumb, the slack, or bight, falling to the side. The romal, a long thong attached to the point where the reins join and used as a switch by the rider, may be carried under the right palm as it rests on the thigh. In the standard grip the hand should be just forward

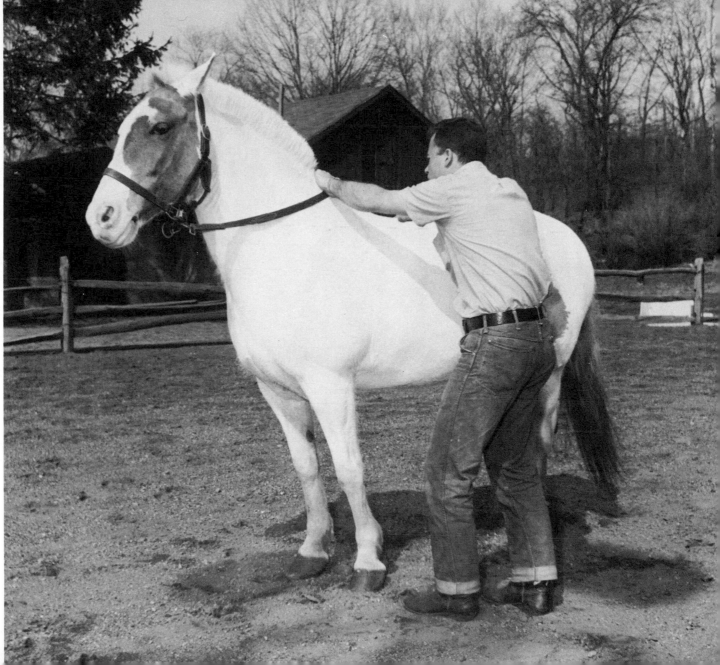

Mounting bareback: first step

Mounting bareback: second step

Mounting bareback: mount completed

of the horn, in the California grip directly above the horn.

To begin walking, nudge the horse with your legs, relax the reins a little, not by letting go of them but by merely moving your hands an inch or two forward. If he doesn't move, tap him with your heels a bit. As he begins to walk, concentrate on maintaining your balance and posture, on keeping your legs close to the horse and keep heels down with pressure on them.

As your horse moves along, keep direct contact with his mouth through the reins. This does not mean jerking or hauling on them, rather "feeling" through them. Let him walk a few hundred feet, then stop him by applying moderate pressure on the reins. While you're stopped, try standing up in the stirrups a couple of times. This will give you a feel for the trotting motion which comes up later.

Start walking again. If you're in a ring or corral, the horse will turn of his own accord. But you should be able to guide him on all occasions. While he's moving, try turning him and going in the opposite direction. Turn him toward the center of the ring by pulling on the rein that will turn his head in that direction and letting up on the other. In other words, turn the horse's head and the rest of him follows. Also turn your own head in the same direction to make sure the way is clear. This little movement will be reflected in your balance and felt by the horse, further guiding him.

Pulling the horse's head, or "plowing," as it is called by judges, is not the approved way of turning, but for the beginner it accomplishes the purpose. As you gain confidence, you should learn to turn your horse by merely leaning your hand or hands in the direction you wish to go. Actually the rein you have been pulling on to turn the horse's head will go slack and the opposite rein will touch his neck halfway between head and shoulder. This signal will turn the horse, as it is part of his training and is called neck reining. It is particularly important in Western riding, and stock horses turn almost instantly on the signal, quicker and easier than by plowing.

For practice, turn your horse to the left and right, turn him in circles, turn him in figure-eights, all at the walk, remembering always to sit erect, head up, eyes ahead, knees tight, heels down and the balls of your feet in the stirrups. Also, remember to turn your head when you want to turn your horse.

You don't often need to back up, but when you do, it must be done from a standstill. Apply even pressure on the reins and be prepared for the horse to shift his weight from hindquarters to forequarters. To stop backing, merely let up on the reins.

Now you know how to mount, dismount, hold the reins English or Western style, adjust the stirrups, the proper seats for each, how to walk your horse, stop him and back him up. Think about all these things.

Establish them clearly in your mind. Practice them until they become automatic.

Posting to the trot and sitting to the jog are next. Both are the same, only the English rider does the former and the Western rider the latter.

To learn to post, ask the stable boy or instructor for a horse that trots well. There is quite a variation and you might as well learn as easily as possible.

The trot is a two-beat gait. A front foot and the opposite rear foot strike the ground together. The horse's rear leg propels him forward until the other front foot and opposite rear foot strike the ground together. All this is very simple, but as the horse's hindquarters drive ahead he goes up to the point where all four feet are off the ground. Obviously the horse's back is then at a higher point than when a pair of his feet are on the ground. This means that if you simply sit on the saddle as the horse trots, you are thrown up a couple of inches, then bounce back down again. If you don't think so, just try it. While your horse is walking, push him a little faster until he breaks into a trot and then try sitting there in an English saddle.

The reason Western riders sit out the trot or jog is that the stock horse is shorter, closer-coupled, and his trot is more of a shuffle without the action or springiness of a rangier horse. Also a jog is done slowly. In a Western Horsemanship class there is never the command "Jog on!" which would require speed and be very uncomfortable for the rider. When the Western rider wants a little more speed he pushes his horse into the slow lope.

Posting is merely a way of avoiding the bounce that comes from the horse's thrusting forward. It's only a matter of timing and provides excellent exercise, but when overdone it can become tiring. (That's why the Tennessee Walker was developed.) The reason we suggested standing in the stirrups earlier was for you to get the feel of posting, which comes only from pushing yourself up and settling down in rhythm with the gait. As the horse trots, you can easily feel the one-two beat as his feet strike the ground—one-two, one-two, one-two . . . You must time yourself so you are at the top of your rise at one, seated at two, top of your rise at one, seated at two, etc. Thus while you're in the middle of going up and down, the horse will have his feet off the ground and the thrust which pushes him forward and upward and makes you bounce will be absorbed by the pivoting action of your body on its knees.

The best way to learn is to trot slowly, count the rhythmic one-two beat of the gait, and as you're bounced off the saddle, push up, then let yourself settle down: push up, settle down, push up, settle down; one at the top, two sitting down, one at the top, two sitting down, etc. Coordinate your body with the rhythm of the gait and you'll soon be posting perfectly. The faster the horse trots, the faster you must post: the slower he trots, the slower you post. If you find yourself losing balance occasionally, it's usually because you don't keep your knees firm enough against the horse to make them act as firm pivots. From the knees down your legs should not move. Your thighs do the lifting, your hips the bending. You use a lot of muscles in posting.

As previously explained, the Western rider sits out the jog. He bounces a little, and over a long period of time it would be uncomfortable, but the jog is not a working gait of the stock horse. It isn't used very much, except in Western equitation and pleasure-horse classes. When doing the jog you should keep your body as erect as possible and your seat low enough in the saddle so no daylight shows. This fault one of the judges looks for.

In posting the trot you cannot keep erect throughout. Going up and coming down you must bend slightly forward to maintain balance, but at the top of your rise and as you meet the saddle you should be absolutely erect. This snapping into erectness with each stride is what makes the posted trot a beautiful gait. When it is done sloppily it is nothing. Practice at a slow trot and gradually work up speed.

The last of the three major gaits is the canter, or lope, again the former English, the latter Western, both terms stand for the same movement, and this time both groups do the same thing. They "sit" the gait and enjoy its invigorating rhythm. The lope of the stock horse must be seen and ridden to be appreciated. It is a slow, almost effortless movement of very little leg action, easy to sit to and tireless to horse and rider. It is the great working gait of the Western horse.

The canter is a pleasurable gait because of its rolling rhythmic movement. It's wise to ask for a mount that canters well because again there is great variation. Horses will break into a canter from a walk but more easily from a trot. The important thing to do is relax and flow with the motion. You must still keep the horse collected, that is, be in "feeling" contact with his mouth. If you don't, he is apt to pick up speed and start flying. The rhythm will be the same, only you'll want to hug your legs tightly to his body for more support and stability. If a horse ever starts to run away with you, don't lean forward. That only encourages him. Lean backward, thrust your legs forward for leverage and *pull on those reins.* If you still can't stop him, try to run him in a circle.

When you're out pleasure riding, it's wise to vary the gaits often. This provides practice as well as variety. Always leave the stable at a walk so that the circulation in the horse's legs and especially his feet has a chance to increase slowly. Bring him in at a walk so that the circulation has a chance to slow down. A horse must always be warmed up before any strenuous exercise and cooled out afterward, or he will founder.

Don't ride with crazy riders. You'll never learn any-

When you lay your saddle down, stand it on end.

Photo: Dick Spohn

Keep your tack clean.

thing and may end up injured. A horse is a big animal. Don't underestimate his strength.

Try some exercises to strengthen your ankles and legs when you first start in. For the ankles, point the toe out and rotate in large circles, keeping the rest of your leg in position, ankles rolled over, toes turned out and hands in front as if holding the reins.

Don't ride too close to the horse in front of you. Many don't like it and will kick. When in a group, don't cluck to your horse to speed him up. It may unexpectedly start someone else's off. There must be courtesy in riding. This is what makes it safe and pleasurable. You should extend it at all times and expect to have it extended in return.

Don't mount a horse on the down side of a hill. Turn him around and gain the advantage. Also, if you ever dismount by yourself and the horse, wanting to catch up with the group or hurry home, refuses to stand still to let you remount, forget the right rein but take a short hold on the left, put your foot in the stirrup and, as you start to swing up, pull hard on that left rein. The horse, in trying to move ahead, will turn right into you and you'll swing up and over with ease.

Remember that all horses are different. After you become fairly proficient in riding, change mounts frequently. This will teach you how to handle various types, how to tell easy- and rough-gaited horses often at sight. There are all kinds, and the best way to learn is by trying them. Horsemanship is common sense and experience, but no matter how far along the road you are, there's always more to be learned.

A rider is one who merely rides a horse. A horseman is one who is able to get any movement from his mount with no apparent effort, and both he and the horse appear relaxed and comfortable at all times. This is the goal to aim for.

18.
Owning
your own horse

THE MORE YOU BECOME INVOLVED IN THE HORSE WORLD the more you will want to own your own horse. It means riding without the trouble of borrowing a friend's horse or the expense of going to a stable and renting a tired nag, or one that has had so much heaving and hauling on his mouth that he is unmanageable. Once you have your own horse you can train him to your ways, compete with him and enjoy him most thoroughly.

Before you buy a horse, you must realize the responsibility involved. He is completely dependent on you for food, cleanliness and health. When he is being ridden and worked he must be fed twice a day, once a day if

Buying a horse at an auction

he has a pasture to graze in. He must be watered, his stall must be cleaned daily and he must be groomed. Not all, but a lot of your spare time will be consumed in this work, so you should use him enough to make your investment and effort worthwhile.

Also, you must figure the expenses involved. There is the initial cost of the horse—from $100 for a half-broken Western cow pony on up to the sky for a registered champion. For $300 to $500 you should find a good one, and it will be worth the extra because he'll eat no more than a poor one.

Another expense is tack, which can often be bought right along with the horse. Even though it's used it serves the purpose. The cheapest new bridle, saddle and halter will run $75, and it goes on up to several hundred. A sheet and blanket will cost another $25. Buckets, pitchfork, shovel, grain measure, grooming tools and tack-cleaning gear another $25.

A horse consumes a considerable amount of hay and grain during the course of a year. Also there's bedding for the stall. Pasturing your horse will keep food expenses down, but you have to give him hay in any event, and grain if you work him. Count on $200 to $350 annually for this, depending on where you live in the country. There will be other expenses—shoeing every six weeks, $5 for resetting, $10 to $15 for new ones, veterinary bills another $50 annually.

If you don't have the facilities for keeping a horse and have to board him out, this will run from $50 to $100 a month depending upon where you live and the service you require. In ascending order of cost, the horse can be pastured, rough-boarded (some grain feeding), stable-boarded (feed and daily grooming) and hunter-boarded (with full care). Veterinary bills and shoeing are extra in all cases.

All this is not to discourage you from buying, only to make you aware of what you're getting into. The best way to enjoy riding is to own a horse, and if you're still ready to go ahead, the next step is to decide what kind suits your purpose. All the registered breeds have been discussed, so you should have an idea of what each one specializes in and what he looks like. Besides registered horses, there are probably two or three times as many unregistered horses available. They sell a lot more cheaply and often have better dispositions. Size, gait and appearance will vary widely, but a grade animal or stock horse will be tougher, more free from disease, able to take the summer heat and winter cold better and require less pampering than a purebred.

If you buy a registered horse, make certain that it's eligible to show in the breed shows around your area. There are four Quarter Horse registries, three Pinto registries, three Appaloosa registries and two Palomino registries, all of which has led to confusion and unnecessary rivalry. For example, if you buy a Pinto in California, chances are that you can't enter it at a breed

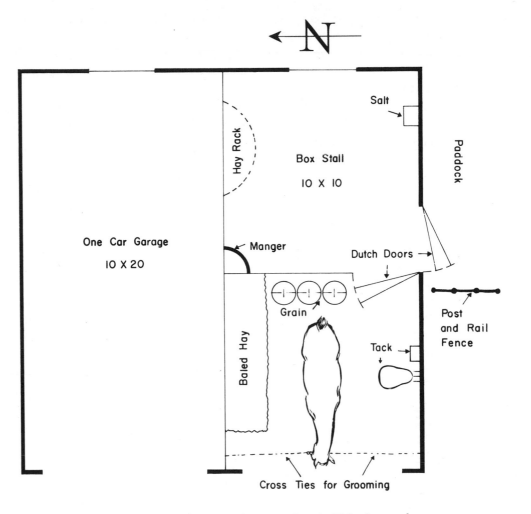

N

Salt

Hay Rack

Box Stall

10 X 10

Paddock

One Car Garage

10 X 20

Manger

Dutch Doors →

Grain

Baled Hay

Post
and Rail
Fence

Tack →

Cross Ties for Grooming

Conversion of two-car garage into complete facilities for one horse

show in Connecticut. The horse will have been registered by a group not recognized by the group putting on the show. Find out what the registry is before you buy.

As for the sex of the horse, a gelding is by far the best for the beginner. A stallion requires too much experience to handle. A mare can be highstrung and temperamental, either by nature or by seasons. Some people buy a mare in foal, use her as a riding horse after the foal is born, then resell her later. But a foal takes three years before it's usable.

Be sure to get a horse that fits you. Maybe that sounds silly, but if you're tall you should have a horse on the large side, otherwise you will find it awkward and overly tiring trying to post rapidly to a small horse's quick gaits. The reverse is also true. A short person finds a big horse more difficult to handle. Balance is harder to maintain, everything is out of proportion.

Before you buy a horse, try to get him on trial for a few days so you can see what he's like, whether he's headshy, leads easily and is mannerly around the stable. Try riding him alone and with other horses. This will give you an idea of his manners. A long, rangy horse is usually rough-gaited and a hard keeper. A short-coupled horse, no matter what his height, is an easy keeper and inclined to have smoother gaits. Always remember to check a horse's vision. Simply brush a hand at each eye and make sure he blinks.

If you can't have him on trial, be sure at least to ride him. Warm him up, then run him a couple of minutes to see how his breathing is. If he sounds like a porpoise sucking air, he's windbroken and not much good for anything but slow, easy riding.

The old expression, "Never look a gift horse in the mouth," doesn't apply when you're buying. Maybe you can't tell his age by his teeth, but a good veterinarian can. And it's certainly worth the $5 or $10 fee to have a vet check a prospective horse for splints, bowed tendons, ring bone and other defects that make a horse unsound and consequently useless.

In recent years tranquilizers have been used on horses to good advantage and purpose, but there is always the cheat who pacifies the unruly animal momentarily just to sell him. This is another reason for having a horse on trial.

Where to buy a horse? If you have enough money you can go to a reliable breeder and be relatively sure of not getting stuck. He has a reputation to maintain.

You can buy at one of the many public auctions held constantly throughout the country. You may or may not save money. You may or may not get stuck. You won't have a chance to try him out but you'll never forget bidding him in. If you buy at an auction, look the stock over beforehand. Remember the sound advice the old gypsy gave his son: "Look at the horse's head first. If you like it, look at his legs. If you like them, you can put up with what's in-between." A drooping lower lip, hollows over the eyes, or too docile an expression are signs of age; also, scars or patches of white hair on the body, particularly where the saddle or girth fits. A horse's lips should meet evenly when viewed from the side. That means his teeth meet squarely inside. If they don't meet right, he can't chew his food, won't fatten and may be old.

Another place to buy is from a local stable or riding school. Here you can usually have a thorough look at one and try him out, but make sure he hasn't been abused by too much hacking.

The best time of year to buy a horse is in the fall. Summer camps are closing and unloading their stock. Students going away to college for the first time can't keep their favorite Saddler or junior hunter. A lot of people won't "winter" a horse through, but simply buy it in the spring and sell again in the fall. With a little looking you can usually pick up a good horse. Remember, it pays to look at a couple of hundred and be satisfied rather than buy the first one and regret it.

After you've bought your horse, you need a stable to keep him in, assuming that you want him at home. A box stall where the horse is loose is the best, ten feet by ten feet for the average mount, twelve by twelve if he's a big hunter. A standing stall with the horse tied is perfectly adequate, provided there is good ventilation without drafts and a pitched floor so he has dry standing.

Most agricultural experts recommend clay floors, but most horsemen prefer dirt. It's cheaper and provides natural drainage where clay doesn't. Some stables use cement floors that are well pitched, but then a thick bedding must be kept. Often two-by-six planks are laid $\frac{1}{2}$ inch apart over concretelike duck boards, and this provides an excellent floor. Straw, peatmoss, peanut shells or wood shavings may be used for bedding, but not hay, as the horse will try to eat it.

The Department of Agriculture has excellent plans available for light-horse barns. Also contact your county agent or the extension agricultural engineer at most state agricultural colleges. For the rural or suburban resident with a couple of acres and a two-car garage the adjoining plan is a very neat and compact arrangement for a horse stall, done with modified conversion. Always try to face the entrance door south so the sun will reach inside the stall a little each day and dry it out.

A paddock or small corral is a necessity if it can be arranged. One of the worst things a horse can do is stand idle in the stall for long periods. It leads to bad habits like cribbing (chewing wood), kicking and weaving (a rhythmical shifting of the weight from one foot to the other). In a small paddock, about thirty by fifty feet, he can get some exercise, fresh air and sunshine. On an acre or two of land he will thrive as well as get some good grazing.

Be careful of your fences around the paddock. If you

use wire, there should be a white rail along the top so the horse can see it easily. Rail fences are preferable. Have the manure pile convenient, but not near the entrance to the horse's stall because it will draw flies. Be sure there are no sharp projections either in the stall or along the fences—they will surely injure him.

Provide the stall with a sturdy metal corner manger, also a hay rack. It's not necessary to keep water in front of the horse, but offer him a bucketful at least twice a day, morning and night. In your combination feed-and-tack room, stack the baled hay against one wall right to the ceiling and use it as necessary. Keep your oats or other feed in large metal garbage cans with a spring running from the handles through the top to keep the lid down tight and the rats out.

Store your saddle on a wall mount, which is merely two stout, smooth boards nailed together at a 90-degree angle and projecting horizontally from the wall. Hang your bridle by the crown on a round fixture or can, not a nail or peg. As soon as you come in from riding and remove the bridle, jounce the lower part in a pail of water so the bit will be washed. This will save a lot of cleaning later. If you've got the time, wipe off the whole bridle with a damp sponge and a little saddle soap. Then clean it immediately. Do the same with the saddle. Always wipe off the underside so the horse sweat doesn't dry on and cake.

If there's any mud on the tack, wash it off quickly.

It's twice as easy when it's fresh. If you are caught in a rain and your tack gets soaked, put a little neatsfoot oil on it afterwards. Saddle pads must be kept clean, and be sure the pad is dry when you use it or the horse will develop back sores.

If your horse comes in muddy, sponge him off with warm water as best as possible, especially his legs and underside. Then put a blanket over him and make sure his stall is not drafty.

Keep his stall clean and dry. It takes effort, but the horse will be healthier in the long run. Damp floors subject the horse to a fungus infection of the feet called thrush. It comes only from neglect. If the horse's feet are kept clean with a hoof pick and the stable floor is dry, it will never occur. When the straw is damp but not soiled, it can be tossed outside in the sun, dried, fluffed up and reused.

In winter, when horses cannot be ridden, many people pasture them and provide only a shed for shelter. Their coats grow thick, but in a reasonably moderate climate with plenty of hay and a little grain they do very well and require a minimum of care. Ponies, particularly Shetlands, are famous for their winter hardiness.

As for feeding your horse, remember he has a simple stomach and can't handle large quantities of roughage at one time. He should be well-fed while he is being used, then "roughed" through the winter months on a poorer diet. Good pastures are the cheapest feed for horses and supply many of the essential vitamins, minerals and protein needed. Working horses should not be fed all the hay they can eat. Too much causes labored breathing and quick tiring while at work. In the spring, when you start in riding or training your horse, cut down on the hay and increase the grain. The best hay is timothy mixed with alfalfa and clover. It should be free of mold, unfrozen and as dust-free as possible.

Ten Rules for Feeding

1. When planning a good ration for your horse, watch his condition and his droppings. When the manure becomes hard and dry, give an occasional feeding of bran mash or green grass. Whenever grass is available the horse should have some.
2. If the horse is thin but is getting more than enough feed, check for worms or bad teeth. The latter may need filing, or "floating."
3. Don't feed grain to a hot horse. Hay won't hurt him.
4. Don't work a horse immediately after feeding; if you must work him immediately, cut his feed in half.
5. Don't give an overly tired horse a full feed of grain.
6. Don't let the horse bolt his grain. If he does, put a smooth rock or two in his manger.
7. Never feed the horse moldy or dirty feed.
8. If it takes your horse longer than 25 to 30 minutes to clean up his grain, cut down on his feed.
9. When your horse has colic, call the veterinarian. Symptoms: pawing the ground, lying down, rolling, and nosing his belly. Causes: overeating, eating while fatigued, working soon after eating, watering while exhausted and wind-sucking.
10. Don't let your horse eat frosted clover. It's often fatal.

The most popular grain for horses is oats, but select your grain on the basis of economy, the same as hay. If oats are more expensive in your area, use corn. It's a heavy, highly concentrated feed, so you can use about 15 percent less than oats, and a little linseed meal or wheat bran should be fed with it. On the average, 6 to 8 pounds of grain a day will keep a horse while working, more if he's a large animal or under heavy training, less if he gets too frisky. In many areas, well-balanced, prepared horse feeds are available for only a few cents more per hundred pounds than grains, in which case it pays to use them and not bother with mixing your own.

A good way to divide the hay ration is one-third in the morning and two-thirds at night, the grain evenly morning and night. You can water before, during or after feeding, but be consistent about it. Be sure to keep salt in front of the horse at all times, either in a wall rack or a chunk of rock salt in the manger. If the horse is pastured, he should have access to a revolving block.

Grooming a horse is an important function in keeping him. It's your way of keeping him clean and presentable. More than that, it gets rid of body waste exuded through the skin, and dirt that blocks this process. It also acts as a stimulant to digestion and makes him feel better.

Horses that are worked hard and fed grain should be groomed every day, at least twice a week for any stabled horse. The more often you groom him, even if only five minutes a day, the better his coat will be. Set up cross-ties that will snap to each side of the horse's halter and keep his head steady, and consequently his body. You'll need a dandy brush which is big and stiff, a curry comb, body brush, rub rag like a cheap bath towel, a mane comb and hoof pick.

Start at the horse's head and work toward his tail. Go over his face and head with the dandy brush, then curry his neck, shoulders and body on back to his tail. The curry comb fits in one hand, the body brush in the other. As you loosen the dirt and dandruff with the curry, brush it away with the body brush. Those spots where the horse is sensitive to the curry can be brushed. Don't curry bony spots or anywhere below the knees. Brush them with the dandy brush. Develop the habit of crossing in front of your horse to work on the other side, not walking behind him. When you're finished, comb out his mane and tail.

This process of grooming has been going on for a couple of thousand years and takes fifteen to thirty minutes to do properly. Now our gadget society has come up with a real timesaver—a portable vacuum cleaner with a curry-brush attached to the nozzle. It does a great job in half the time and is certainly worth the investment.

When you're finished grooming, sponge out the nostrils, the tail area and sheath. Then apply a little hoof dressing, which not only makes the hoofs look better but keeps them from cracking and splitting. Then your horse is ready to ride.

In summer it's a good idea to give him a bath once in a while if the sun is out and the weather is warm. Use warm water, either from a hose or by the bucket. You can get a lot of water off with a sweat-scraper, then use towels or rags for the rest. Walk him a little and don't put him away in a draft. Incidentally, a good supply of cheap bath towels is essential. You use them at every turn, and they can be washed easily.

Keeping a horse entails some work and expense, as you can see. If you are the kind of person who will not care for him consistently and properly, by all means don't buy one. But if you love horses and make the effort to keep yours properly, he will reward you a hundred times over. There is something basic about owning a horse that goes deeper than owning a sports car or some other fine mechanical gadget. He is flesh and blood combined with spirit, honesty and nobleness, a welcome relief from our harassing world of automation and massive destruction. Perhaps this is why the horse is not really obsolete today. Man, in thirsting for these higher qualities, finds them easily in the horse, his oldest partner, ally and friend in time of trouble.

19.
Twenty-five rules for safety

OCCASIONALLY YOU READ OR HEAR ABOUT SOMEONE WHO has been hurt while handling horses. Most of these accidents could be prevented by learning a few rules of safety and in this, the last chapter, we would like to list twenty-five such rules assembled by Dr. Russell E. Smith, Professor of Veterinary Science at the University of Massachusetts, Amherst, Massachusetts.

1. Always speak to a horse before touching him. Most horses will jump and some will kick when startled. Let him know that you are approaching.
2. Whenever possible, approach a horse from the front. If moving around the rear of the horse, keep a hand firmly on him so he knows where you are. Do not tickle him.

3. The closer you stand to a horse, the less likely you will be kicked; you may be shoved away, but not hurt.
4. Never tease your horse or allow others to tease or abuse him. He may develop habits which are hard to unlearn.
5. Learn simple means of restraint, such as cross-tying in the open and holding up a front foot.
6. Learn the safe and proper way to lift and hold feet, particularly hind feet.
7. Use a long lead strap when leading. Snap chain over nose if horse is difficult to control.
8. Keep both hands on lead strap. If horse goes up, release hand nearest to halter so you can stay on the ground.
9. Remember that the horse is stronger than you. You cannot outpull him, so outthink him. A quick snap on the lead strap will usually remind him of his manners.
10. Walk beside your horse when leading, not ahead or behind him.
11. Keep leads and longe lines off the ground so he does not get his feet entangled.
12. When leading into a box stall, turn the horse around facing the door before releasing the lead strap.
13. Horses by nature are kind and gentle. However, when full fed and getting little exercise, they can work up a little steam. Do not try to starve your horse into submission, but handle and work him regularly to avoid an accumulation of bursting energy.
14. Horses can be frightened by unusual objects and noises. Anticipate such fright and steady your horse.
15. Keep tack in good condition and properly adjusted to horse. Replace worn parts with new ones. Check bridle, stirrup leathers and girths especially. Use safety catches for stirrup leathers on English tack.
16. Adjust saddle carefully so it does not slip while mounting. Take up girth again after horse is led out of stable.
17. Mount in the open and away from hard surfaces or rocks. If horse sidesteps, you have a softer landing.
18. If horse is too full of steam, work on a longe line a few minutes before riding.
19. Keep your horse under control at all times. He is working for *you*, not vice versa. Adjust your gait or speed to the terrain. Keep off pavement, and generally follow the rules for the safe operation of an automobile.
20. Walk uphill and down. If riding in groups on the trail, keep your distance from the horse in front, and be alert for overhead obstacles.
21. If your horse is frightened by an obstacle, dismount and lead him by it.

22. When a horse is frightened and attempts to run, keep him turned in a circle in one direction, and tighten the circle until he stops.

23. You are the brains of the outfit. Avoid holes and obstacles where the horse and yourself can be hurt.

24. More people fall off horses than are thrown or bucked off. A sudden change of direction or an insecure seat while posting the trot contribute to the beginner's falls. Develop a secure seat and do not blame the horse for your lack of experience.

25. Manners and suitability to the experience of the owner are prime qualities in any horse. Above all, know your horse, and make sure your manners are at least equal to his.

Index

Chase Me (Thoroughbred), 21-22
Chicago International (horse show), 77
Children, horses for: Appaloosas, 98, 102; Galicenos, 117; Norwegian Duns, 117; Quarter Horses, 62; Tennessee Walkers, 86. *See also* Ponies
Chincoteague ponies, 122-23
Citation (Thoroughbred), 29, 35
Civil War, horses in, 75, 87
Claiming races, 27, 28
Cleveland Bays, 22, 40
Clothes for riding, 147
Cold blood, defined, 10
Collection, defined, 76
Colleges: equine teaching at, 2; polo at, 127
Colors of horses, 8; albinos, 104, 109, 112-13. *See also Silks; specific breeds*
Connemara ponies, 121-22
Copenhagen (Appaloosa), 99
*Copperbottom (Tennessee Walker), 75, 87
Cornell University, 26
Count Fleet (Thoroughbred), 29
Coyote hunting, 40
Cutting, 138; by Appaloosas, 102; by Arabians, 18; by Quarter Horses, 60

Daily Double, 35
Dan Patch (Standardbred), 46
Darley Arabian (Thoroughbred sire), 22, 42
Darn Safe (Standardbred), 48
De Lancey, Col. James, 66, 68-69
Delaware Park (Del. race track), 33
Denmark (Thoroughbred), 22, 75, 87

Diamond Hal (Standardbred), 48
Distaff Big Three, 33
Doble, Budd, 45, 48
Dreitzler, Mr. and Mrs. Ralph, 115
Dressage: by Arabians, 18; by Lippizaners, 115
Du Quoin, Ill., 45
Dude ranches, 91

Eclipse (Thoroughbred), 22
Ellsworth, Rex, 10, 33-34
Eohippus, 5-6, 122
*Epinard (Thoroughbred), 22
Equipoise (Thoroughbred), 22
Equitation classes in horse shows, 134, 140
Ethan Allen (Morgan), 44, 70

Fair Play (Thoroughbred), 23
Feeding a horse, 170-73; expenses of, 166
Fillies, defined, 8
Find (Thoroughbred), 35
First Landing (Thoroughbred), 35
Flat racing, *see* Racing; Racing by Thoroughbreds
Fleming, Vic, 47
Flora Temple (trotter), 45
Florence, Ariz., 144
Foals: defined, 8; late foals, 8; training of, 30
Fox hunting, 39-40, 122; hunter division in horse shows, 134
Fox-Trot Horses, 113
Futurity races, 28-29

Gaines' Denmark (American Saddler sire), 75

Gaits of horses, 10; of American Saddlers, 75-77; of Arabians, 15; and learning to ride, 155-60; of Missouri Fox-Trotters, 113; pacing vs. trotting, 48; of Palominos, 106; of Paso Finos, 116; seven-gaited horses, 88; of Tennessee Walkers, 84-86, 88, 91
Galiceno Horse, 117
Gallant Fox (Thoroughbred), 29
Galophone (Standardbred), 48
Geldings: best for beginners, 168; defined, 8
George Wilkes (Standardbred), 44, 52, 88
Glendale Course (Va. race track), 36
Glendenning, George, 110
Godolphin Arabian (Godolphin Barb), 22, 23, 42, 69
Goldsmith's Maid (Standardbred), 45-46, 48
Good Time (Standardbred), 48
Goshen, N.Y., 45
"Grade," use of term, 10
Grand National (England), 36, 37
Greece, ancient horsemanship in, 13-14, 133
Greyhound (Standardbred), 44, 46, 70
Grooming a horse, 173
Gussie Wilkes (Standardbred), 51

Hackney Horses, 22, 40
Hackney ponies, 120
Halter classes in horse shows, 140
Hambletonian (race), 45
Hambletonian (Standardbred), 22, 43-45, 88
Hand, defined, 8
Handicap races, 28